W9-ADS-353

OLLIE
DABBOUS
ESSENTIAL

BLOOMSBURY PUBLISHING
Bloomsbury Publishing Plc
50 Bedford Square, London, WC1B 3DP, UK
29 Earlsfort Terrace, Dublin 2, Ireland

BLOOMSBURY, BLOOMSBURY PUBLISHING and the Diana logo are trademarks of
Bloomsbury Publishing Plc.

First published in Great Britain in 2021

Text © Ollie Dabbous, 2021
Photographs © Joakim Blockström, 2021

Ollie Dabbous and Joakim Blockström have asserted their right under the Copyright, Designs
and Patents Act, 1988, to be identified as author and photographer, respectively, of this work.

For legal purposes the Acknowledgements on p.313 constitute an extension of this copyright page.

All rights reserved. No part of this publication may be reproduced or transmitted in any form or
by any means, electronic or mechanical, including photocopying, recording, or any information
storage or retrieval system, without prior permission in writing from the publishers.

Bloomsbury Publishing Plc does not have any control over, or responsibility for, any third-party
websites referred to or in this book. All internet addresses given in this book were correct at the
time of going to press. The author and publisher regret any inconvenience caused if addresses
have changed or sites have ceased to exist, but can accept no responsibility for any such changes.

A catalogue record for this book is available from the British Library.

Library of Congress Cataloguing-in-Publication data has been applied for.

ISBN: HB: 978-1-4088-4395-6; eBook: 978-1-4088-4396-3

10 9 8 7 6 5 4 3 2 1

Editor: Rowan Yapp
Project Editor: Lucy Bannell
Designer: Dave Brown at APE
Photographer: Joakim Blockström
Food Stylist: Ollie Dabbous
Prop Stylist: Jennifer Kay
Indexer: Vanessa Bird

Printed and bound in China by C&C Offset Printing Ltd.

To find out more about our authors and books visit www.bloomsbury.com and sign up for
our newsletters.

OLLIE DABBOUS ESSENTIAL

PHOTOGRAPHY BY
JOAKIM BLOCKSTRÖM

BLOOMSBURY PUBLISHING
LONDON • OXFORD • NEW YORK • NEW DELHI • SYDNEY

6

The best food is always the simplest, whether you are cooking it at home or eating in a restaurant. And the simplest food is always the most sophisticated. With the recipes in this book, I want to capture the essence of each ingredient through what I call 'boldly refined' home cooking: simple techniques, good taste and concise ingredients underpin every dish. The recipes themselves are stripped back to flavour combinations that work together without superfluous fuss and, on the rare occasion that one is slightly more involved, it is always worth the effort; there is a reason why every component is on the plate. Whether it's a twist on a classic or a more contemporary dish, these recipes will help you to elevate the everyday into something special. I hope you not only want to eat this food, but want to make it again and again.

All the recipes are accessible to anyone who enjoys good food, even if you have no confidence about how to cook it. So put your trust in me. I hope that you can grow as a cook with this book, as my explanations (often just applied common sense) help you to understand how to cook great food at home and – importantly – to hone your intuition around ingredients and how to cook them, so you know how to get a recipe just right. I want you to feel proud every time you serve one of these dishes.

Confidence is the greatest asset you can possess in the kitchen; it empowers you to do more with fewer ingredients. And, in fact, the less confidence you have in the kitchen, the less you should over-analyse what you are doing. Instead, taste your food: does it taste right? A good palate only comes with experience. So consciously break things down while you are tasting a dish: does it need more acid? More salt? More fat? Or even – as is sometimes the case for dressings – a pinch of sugar?

When you make a simple salad, for instance – and there are plenty in these pages – you need pops of flavour and acidity from citrus or vinegar, the sharpness of a dressing combined with crunchy, verdant leaves. I like to serve a salad at the start of a meal to get you salivating, with flavours that wake up your palate with a jolt. At the other end of the spectrum lies something such as vanilla ice cream, a soft, melting, rounded white cloud that tastes exactly as it looks in a wonderful symbiosis of texture and taste. Its gentle flavours should be like a familial embrace at the end of a meal, rather than anything too demanding or arresting.

My grandmother on my mum's side was of the war generation and I cooked with her from the age of six. We always had a proper teatime at her house and I will never forget her egg custard tarts and cakes. As you'll see from the recipes in this book, I still like puddings, and it is this comforting nature of home cooking that appeals to me the most. There is something intrinsically soothing about simple food done well. Home cooking has a joy that is quite distinct from the more intricate pleasures of restaurant food. My restaurant dishes have to be exciting, theatrical and sexy, whereas the delight of home cooking often lies in gentle, nuanced and subtle melding of flavours, in slow-cooked braises or soft puddings.

Home cooking is a labour of love, and it's a way of showing affection, too. Since becoming a father, I've felt passionately that eating well at home is something we need to learn to do again as a society. I would love it if we could reintroduce home economics in school, for instance, because if kids learn to cook, they will also learn to respect the process and the produce. Good cooking can be enjoyed by all, irrespective of income: it's a true democratic luxury.

It is *essential* that everyone is able to cook good food at home and to provide a nutritious, delicious meal for themselves and their loved ones. Gathering around the table is both a sign and a symptom of civilisation. A society that eats well is a civilised society with a healthy population, with more mutual respect. When people cook and eat well, they tend to have better relationships and are less likely to hide behind screens, mindlessly absorbing the inane while real life passes them by. The ripple effect of good home cooking is enormous; we ignore it at our peril.

RESTRAINT

The recipes in this book are economical, on purpose. Restraint in the kitchen invariably produces a more sophisticated result, and restraint often comes with confidence. Home cooking shouldn't be 'clever', just authentic, delicious and honest. There's something wonderfully inspirational about economy in food. If you are limited in the ingredients you use – because you want to cook local produce, or you haven't got great reserves of money – that forces creativity.

It's the best of cooking; the less you need to do to an ingredient to make a delicious plate of food, the more currency that recipe has. The Italian dish *pappa al pomodoro* is the perfect example of this: just garlic, olive oil, tomatoes and bread combining to create something incredibly harmonious. Great home cooking is not about using luxury ingredients, it's about making nourishing food that everyone can afford. I want the recipes in this book to be both democratic and empowering, for everyone to enjoy; there is nothing elitist or off-putting about them.

8

The joy of restraint also lies in its efficiency: simple techniques, fewer ingredients, less time spent in the kitchen… and less washing up.

Eating in restaurants is not a pleasure available to all. In continental Europe, eating well is something that everyone can enjoy, irrespective of the contents of their bank account. There's some amazing peasant food in Italy and France and we can definitely learn from that, though British food often requires a little bit more work from the home cook than does the produce of warmer places. We don't have a Mediterranean climate and our grains and root vegetables need more applied effort to render them delicious: more toil to grow and more labour to prepare.

But we can make amazing dishes with the vegetables and grains that we *do* grow here – such as the carrot tartare you will find in these pages – cooked and dressed with a light touch. A whole generation are producing food based on ingredients grown within miles of their stoves, such as – in Britain – cobnuts or fig leaves. But I want *all* home cooks to celebrate their local produce in the same way, and – where it is called for – to add those ingredients from around the globe that are now available to us all.

I have deliberately created the recipes in this book to be accessible without expensive equipment. A blender is helpful, as are accurate digital scales, a timer and a good kitchen thermometer, so your cooking has the best chance to achieve consistency.

Remember that it's quicker to make the recipes in this book properly, in the way that they have been written, than it is to rectify mistakes at the end of the process that have come about from taking a wrong turn along the way. If you do as the recipe directs, you will achieve a good end result. After all, in the kitchen, it takes the same amount of effort to do something well as it does to do it badly.

INGREDIENTS

You may be thinking that advocating the highest quality ingredients is very easy for me, with all the beautiful produce I have at my fingertips as a restaurant chef. But I also grocery shop for my family. So I know that it's easy to get stuck in a safe but dull routine of going to the same supermarket and buying an identical trolley-load week after week. It takes a bit of effort to look further afield, but if you do, you will never look back.

I'm writing these words during the COVID-19 lockdown of 2020–21, and this time has been an education on lifting those shopping-habit blinkers. Many of us – me included – have discovered amazing produce online that can be sent direct to our homes. Of all the great stuff out there, I recommend targeting first those items that aren't perishable. You really can buy anything to stock up your kitchen cupboards: exotica such as fig leaf oil, smoked sundried tomatoes and yuzu juice, or just the basics such as outstanding olive oils and balsamic vinegars. You only need to visit three or four websites to gather a very contemporary larder of wonderful ingredients. If you've got a well-stocked kitchen with good oils and grains that all keep very well, you can spend more time choosing truly excellent fish, meat or vegetables. And here, too, don't be tempted to rely solely on supermarkets. Visit a fishmonger for fish. Have a look online for meat to order straight from the farm, or cheese from the dairy. And you'll know that your money's going directly to those people who produce the goods, rather than to a middleman.

In the last decade, the variety of exciting food available to us has changed dramatically, but our shopping habits haven't. We find ourselves queuing for mediocrity, when we could have the best produce delivered straight to our door. This means that a disconnect has developed between the way in which we cook at home and the food we can find in restaurants. When we eat out, we expect to see inspiring ingredients on the plate, but somehow we overlook the fact that we can cook with these ingredients at home, too. We don't need to buy the same packets and cans that we've been buying for a decade. I want to help you to make the mental jump to rediscovering a sense of adventure around cooking at home.

Home cooking at its best is comforting, generous and delicious. I love food and I love to eat, and my *essential* compilation of recipes celebrates the best home cooking, while giving you the know-how to make it with restaurant-quality finesse. And you'll enjoy it, too, I promise.

All recipes serve four unless otherwise indicated.

All dairy, eggs and poultry are organic or free-range.

All eggs are medium unless otherwise stated.

All citrus is unwaxed.

All fish and shellfish is sustainable (check www.msc.org for up-to-date lists).

All milk, yogurt and other dairy is full fat.

For suppliers, see page 312.

Please read the recipes from start to finish before you start to cook them.

GRAINS

12

The literal seeds for new life, grains are packed with both carbohydrates and protein: everything they need to fuel a plant's growth, and ours. Grains are the very definition of a staple, once so vital to human existence that they were even used as currency. It is good to see them highly valued once again. Aside from their nutritional benefit to us, they are a bedrock ingredient in the kitchen, used in every country and in every cuisine of the globe. They can be ground into flours for baking or binding, or cooked whole, when their variety of textures are most fully revealed.

It is in their natural, unprocessed state that we can appreciate the individual characteristics of grains the most. When gently simmered and just cooked, whole grains are toothsome, fluffy and moreish, ready to be laced with dressing, toasted in a hot pan, or served as a simple accompaniment to a rich stew.

Grains are incredibly versatile and go well with just about anything. Their nutty taste and pleasing texture are the perfect vehicle for spices such as cinnamon, cloves, bay or star anise, especially in a pilaf. They also work brilliantly with the soft sweetness of baked root vegetables or chestnuts. When served warm, grains are a go-to ingredient in the colder months and need little embellishment to create a nourishing and comforting supper.

While there is no need to add dairy, butter or cream provide richness and luxury in any grain dish, while a scatter of grated salty cheese such as Parmesan can add a delicious savoury kick. In spring and summer, grains are perfect served cold as the base for a salad such as a classic tabbouleh, or mixed with plenty of cooked and raw vegetables, feta cheese and olive oil.

Whenever cooking grains, do read the instructions on the packet, even if you think you know how to treat them, as some need soaking overnight in plenty of water before cooking, whereas others are almost instant. The quick-cook variety of polenta used in this chapter can be made in a matter of minutes, but the unprocessed type takes far longer; bulgur wheat can be cooked simply by pouring over boiling water from a kettle and covering the bowl. Spelt, in contrast, can take close to an hour of simmering to cook to a nutty bite. Each recipe in this chapter demonstrates a different cooking method for each grain: from making a risotto using pearl barley, to creating a simple tray-baked pudding from brown rice.

When simmering grains, there is often little need to add stock; lightly seasoned water is usually perfectly fine, especially if sweated vegetables, herbs or bacon have been added at the start of cooking to impart a lovely flavour and turn the humble grains into a healthy, no-fuss meal. Remember that much of the liquid in which grains are cooked is going to be absorbed by them, so always salt them with a light hand.

Consider the type of dish you want to make before choosing the variety of grain for it. If you want to make something creamy such as risotto, use a starchier grain such as barley or rice, simmer it in less liquid and beat it often to help it to release its starch. If you want a lighter, fluffier result such as a pilaf or broth, choose a grain such as einkorn or spelt, rinse it well to remove the starch, then, as a general rule, cook it in plenty of liquid. (The notable exception is bulgur, which requires only minimal water to rehydrate and become fluffy.)

Take time, too, to consider the volume of liquid in which you are cooking the grains; it is easier to add more liquid if needed than to take it away, and it is worth following exact recipes and ratios so the correct amount is absorbed by the grain. Chia seeds and oats are both soaked from raw to create breakfast dishes in this chapter and are capable of absorbing a vast amount of liquid; I urge you to use the volumes I suggest, even if you think they are too much, as any less may well give an end result that is claggy and clumsy.

Just as all grains behave differently in their natural state, so do the flours made from them. Rye flour is packed with flavour but doesn't have as much integral strength as strong bread flour, so these two are mixed – along with wholemeal flour, for texture – in the blinis in this chapter.

The grains in this chapter are not meant to be an exhaustive list, but rather to provide a basic armoury of recipes and techniques that can be used as a blueprint for any other varieties you may encounter, as well as give you the confidence to experiment with adding a novel grain to your shopping basket.

Grains were once considered left-field and solely for vegetarians. They are now loved the world over and take their place at the centre of our meals and our plates. The seeds of change…

GRANOLA

Granola has healthy connotations, but when you read a recipe for it, the reality is somewhat different. Nevertheless, it's a wonderful showcase for grains. This recipe makes a good amount, but there is no point making any less. Store it in an airtight container to preserve its crunch. You can enjoy this with regular milk, of course, but I think it is even nicer with an almond and coconut milk blend. Granola's variations are endless: you could use dried red fruits and coconut flakes in summer, or dried banana and cocoa nibs in the depths of winter.

Makes 1.5kg

DRY INGREDIENTS

200g sunflower seeds

100g pumpkin seeds

100g poppy seeds

100g pine nuts

100g slivered almonds

300g jumbo porridge oats

200g bran flakes, crushed

1 teaspoon fine sea salt

CARAMEL

120g light brown sugar

60g clear honey

60g maple syrup

60g unsalted butter, chopped

60g virgin rapeseed oil

1 teaspoon ground cinnamon

DRIED FRUIT

50g goji berries

50g dried cranberries

50g golden raisins

———

DRY INGREDIENTS

~ Mix together all the dry ingredients.

CARAMEL

~ Bring all the ingredients for the caramel to the boil in a large saucepan with a pinch of salt, then remove from the heat and mix in the dry ingredients. Leave for 30 minutes.

~ Preheat the oven to 110°C.

~ Spread the granola out on 2 baking trays lined with baking parchment.

~ Cook for 90 minutes, stirring every 30 minutes, until evenly light brown. Remove and transfer to a bowl.

DRIED FRUIT

~ Mix in the dried fruit while the granola is still warm.

~ Leave to cool to room temperature.

TO SERVE

~ Serve in cereal bowls with ice-cold milk, or almond and coconut milk.

CHIA SEEDS IN ALMOND MILK; ROAST PLUMS & CINNAMON

A satisfying start to the morning. All the elements can be made the day before, buying you extra time in bed! The plums can be served warm or cold, as you wish. Chia can be bought in larger supermarkets; the seeds of a plant from the mint family, they are a great source of energy. The trick is to soak them in plenty of liquid and leave enough time for them to rehydrate, as insufficient soaking can lead to a slimy texture, rather than a refreshing one. Don't worry how wet it looks at the start; the seeds absorb more than ten times their weight in liquid. You can substitute another stone fruit, or red berries.

This is delicious scattered with flaked almonds.

CHIA SEEDS

500g almond milk

200g mascarpone

75g caster sugar

1 vanilla pod, split lengthways, seeds scraped out, or 1 teaspoon vanilla extract

70g chia seeds

PLUMS

4 plums, halved and pitted

2 tablespoons clear honey

2 tablespoons olive oil

ASSEMBLE

4 tablespoons thick Greek yogurt

pinch of ground cinnamon

CHIA SEEDS

~ Whisk or blend everything except the seeds together to dissolve the sugar and smooth out the mascarpone, then add the chia seeds. Leave the mixture in the refrigerator to rehydrate for at least 45 minutes, whisking every 5 minutes for the first 15 minutes.

PLUMS

~ Preheat the oven to 160°C.

~ Mix the plums with the honey, olive oil and 2 tablespoons water. Place in a roasting tray cut-side down and cook in the oven for 15 minutes.

~ Remove from the oven and serve warm, or leave to cool to room temperature. (Chill if serving the next day.)

ASSEMBLE

~ Place a plum half in each of 4 dishes, then top evenly with the chia seeds.

~ Spoon over the yogurt, then sprinkle with the cinnamon.

~ Top with another plum half, then drizzle over some of the scarlet plum cooking juices.

BIRCHER MUESLI, SOUR CHERRIES, PISTACHIOS & BUTTERMILK

Bircher muesli is a recipe that isn't hard to get right, but can be even easier to get wrong. It can be too thick or claggy, too sweet, or too stingy with the fruits and nuts. However, this recipe is a vibrant burst of colours, tastes and textures. Best of all, it can be made in advance and keeps well in the refrigerator. Chia seeds are not traditional in a bircher, but they do lighten the result. Soaking the dried fruits overnight along with the grains gives a much better result than adding them at the end, as they soften and plump up in the apple juice.

The variations of this are endless: the recipe here is for the winter months, but you could try pear and walnut in the autumn, or apricot, flaked almonds and fragrant lemon thyme in the summer. The breezy mint lifts the dish with every mouthful. If buttermilk isn't available, simply swap for more yogurt.

MUESLI

250g apple juice

20g porridge oats

20g chia seeds

75g dried sour cherries, halved

25g golden raisins

75g pistachios, plus 4 tablespoons

1 eating apple, coarsely grated, avoiding the core (any variety is fine)

125g thick Greek yogurt

125g buttermilk

finely grated zest and juice of ½ lemon

4 tablespoons pomegranate seeds

4 tablespoons blueberries

ASSEMBLE

4 tablespoons blueberries, halved

4 tablespoons pomegranate seeds

4 tablespoons pistachios

leaves from 4 mint sprigs

_____

MUESLI

~ Mix together the apple juice, oats, chia, cherries and raisins in a bowl and leave overnight to soak and rehydrate. Do not drain.

~ Toast the pistachios: preheat the oven to 170°C. Toast the nuts on a baking tray for 10 minutes until golden. Remove and chop 4 tablespoons.

~ Mix the rest of the cooled nuts and all the remaining ingredients into the bowl with the oats and divide between 4 serving bowls, or chill until needed.

ASSEMBLE

~ Sprinkle the blueberries, pomegranate seeds, reserved chopped pistachios and mint over the muesli and serve.

COCONUT MILK & PALM SUGAR PORRIDGE, DATE & TAMARIND COMPOTE

Porridge is a great example of a simple grain preparation with just a few basic ingredients… but it can be either incredible or disgusting, depending on the skill of the person who made it or the recipe they were following. Here's a few things I've learned: by soaking the oats, you need to cook them with less liquid, giving a lighter, more digestible end result. Always use jumbo oats for a fuller, toothsome texture.

It is obviously fine to use regular milk and sugar here, instead of the coconut milk and palm sugar suggested, if you're feeling less exotic in the morning. There is no need to cook the porridge any longer than stated or it can start to go gloopy; this is because it contains a protein called avenin, similar to gluten.

The compote is a delicious alternative to honey or maple syrup, and will keep well in the refrigerator. It has an almost fudge-like depth of flavour, without the cloying sweetness. Do try this recipe one weekend as it is so simple to make, utterly delicious, and probably unlike any other porridge you have had before.

DATE & TAMARIND COMPOTE

150g pitted dates

1 teaspoon white miso paste

1 tablespoon tamarind paste

60g virgin rapeseed oil

30g flaked almonds, lightly toasted (see page 19)

PORRIDGE

250g jumbo porridge oats

1 teaspoon fine sea salt

45g palm sugar, or soft brown sugar

500g canned coconut milk

____

DATE & TAMARIND COMPOTE

~ In a food processor, blend half the dates with 75g water, the miso and tamarind pastes, then add the virgin rapeseed oil in a stream — still blending — until emulsified. Transfer to a bowl.

~ Chop the remaining dates and mix them in with the flaked almonds.

PORRIDGE

~ Soak the oats in a bowl overnight in 1 litre water.

~ Put the oats into a saucepan with any remaining soaking water and all the rest of the ingredients and bring to the boil. Cook for 5 minutes, stirring, then remove from the heat and allow to cool for a couple of minutes.

TO SERVE

~ Serve the porridge in 4 deep bowls with the compote alongside.

21

WHOLEMEAL BLINIS, SMOKED SALMON

Blinis are unashamedly old-fashioned, to the point of quaintness, but, when freshly made, they are still the best vehicle for showcasing smoked salmon. Warm, light and pillowy, with a light crust from cooking in salted butter, they are wholesome and incredibly moreish. This recipe has a depth of flavour from rye and wholemeal flours, with none of the clagginess you can get with potato blinis. Of course, these are equally good with any other smoked fish.

BLINIS

320g whole milk, warmed to body temperature, or just warm to the touch

10g fresh yeast, or 2 teaspoons fast-action dried yeast

1 teaspoon fine sea salt

1 teaspoon caster sugar

1 tablespoon malt extract

2 eggs, separated

75g plain wholemeal flour

75g strong white bread flour

25g dark rye flour

1 teaspoon baking powder

salted butter, to fry

ASSEMBLE

sliced smoked salmon

lemon wedges

crème fraîche

Pickled onions (see page 304)

BLINIS

~ Pour the warm milk into the bowl of a food mixer. Whisk in the yeast, salt, sugar, malt extract and egg yolks just until everything is dissolved.

~ Add all 3 flours and the baking powder and mix for just a couple of minutes until combined. Cover the bowl with cling film and leave the batter to prove for 2–3 hours.

~ After this time has elapsed, whisk the egg whites to medium peaks, then add a pinch of salt and beat to firm peaks. Fold them into the yeast mixture.

~ Heat a nonstick pan over a medium heat, then add a little salted butter. Take scoops of the blini mix, each about 1 tablespoon, and fry in the pan until light golden. You will need to do this in batches.

~ Flip over and cook on the other sides, then place on a tray to keep warm while you cook the remaining blinis.

ASSEMBLE

~ Lay the salmon, lemon wedges, crème fraîche and pickled onions out, for everyone to help themselves, and serve with the warm blinis. This should feel like a treat.

PICK-ME-UP VEGETABLE & SPELT BROTH

The first time I made pistou soup, it was a revelation to me how such simple ingredients could transform into something so delicious. Using water as a base for soup often gives the best result. Here, the neutrality of water means the flavours of vegetables, oil and herbs are crystal-clear rather than muted by the stale savouriness of a stock cube. Boiling water is also key: quick cooking means the flavours are fresh, not tired.

PESTO

30g basil

30g baby spinach

1 tablespoon toasted pine nuts

½ garlic clove

75g extra virgin olive oil

25g grated Parmesan, plus more to serve

pinch of fine sea salt

pinch of caster sugar

SPELT

100g pearled spelt

6g fine sea salt

BROTH

1 onion, sliced into 8, then cored

1 fennel bulb, halved and finely sliced

2 carrots, halved and finely sliced

2 celery sticks, peeled and finely sliced

50g extra virgin olive oil

1 teaspoon fine sea salt

400g can of butter beans, drained and rinsed (about 200g drained weight)

½ bunch baby radishes (4–5 per person), trimmed, or breakfast radishes, halved and trimmed

leaves from 4 thyme sprigs, chopped

pinch of crushed black pepper

———

PESTO

~ Blend everything for 10 seconds.

SPELT

~ Place everything in a saucepan with 1 litre water, bring to a simmer and cook gently for 40 minutes, or until softened but toothsome. Drain.

BROTH

~ Sweat the vegetables in the oil with the salt, covered, for 5 minutes, or until softened but not coloured. Pour in 1 litre boiling water and cook until tender (about 8 minutes).

~ Add the beans, radishes, spelt, thyme and pepper and check the seasoning.

TO SERVE

~ Stir the pesto into the broth and divide it between 4 warmed bowls. Serve with Parmesan to scatter on top.

BARLEY RISOTTO WITH SUMMER VEGETABLES

26

Though you may associate pearl barley more with autumnal fare, this is a delicious summer dish. It tastes healthy and nourishing and is laden with fresh vegetables. I never tire of it and often make it at home. In colder months, feel free to use pumpkin, chestnuts and kale in place of the summer vegetables here, replace the tomato juice with water or chicken stock and the olive oil with rapeseed. Similarly, swap the basil and parsley for a sprinkle of rosemary or thyme. Do stick to the cooking guidelines and ratios, however, for something toothsome and well-balanced. Barley is more robust than risotto rice, so the dish is more forgiving, but do cook it evenly and over no more than a medium heat.

HERB MASCARPONE

200g mascarpone

50g aged Parmesan, finely grated

10g chopped parsley leaves

10g chopped basil leaves

1 small garlic clove, crushed

6 turns of black pepper

pinch of fine sea salt

TOMATO JUICE

500g cherry tomatoes, halved

2 tablespoons Chardonnay vinegar

1 teaspoon caster sugar

1 teaspoon fine sea salt

RISOTTO

75g extra virgin olive oil

100g (1 large or 2 small) banana shallots, finely chopped

100g (½ bulb) fennel, finely chopped

1 celery stick, peeled of string and finely chopped

200g pearl barley

75g white wine

1 quantity Tomato juice (see left)

1 courgette, halved lengthways, then cut across into 3mm slices on an angle

100g peas, fresh or frozen and defrosted

50g frozen edamame, defrosted

8 breakfast radishes, halved

8 cherry tomatoes, halved

1 quantity Herb mascarpone (see left)

fine sea salt

ASSEMBLE

handful of Kalamata olives, pitted, washed and halved

handful of baby artichokes in oil, drained

handful of pea shoots

handful of rocket

handful of basil leaves

Lemon dressing (see page 294)

Parmesan shavings

HERB MASCARPONE

~ Mix all the ingredients together with a spatula, or in a food mixer.

TOMATO JUICE

~ Mix everything together and leave for 1 hour at room temperature, then blend. Pass it through a sieve.

RISOTTO

~ Heat the olive oil in a wide pan, then add the shallots, fennel and celery and season lightly with salt. Cover and sweat for 5 minutes without colour.

~ Add the barley. Cook for 2 minutes to warm the grains and coat them in oil.

~ Add the wine and reduce it completely, then add 600g water and 1 teaspoon salt and simmer gently, stirring until completely evaporated.

~ Add the tomato juice and continue to cook for another 15 minutes.

~ Once the liquid has largely evaporated and the barley is cooked but retains some texture, add the vegetables and cook for 3 minutes until al dente.

~ Add the herb mascarpone and cook until the liquid is just coating the barley grains: this should only take another couple of minutes.

~ Finally, remove from the heat and leave to rest for 2 minutes.

ASSEMBLE

~ Spoon the risotto on to 4 warmed plates or shallow dishes.

~ Lightly dress the olives, artichokes, pea shoots, rocket and basil with lemon dressing, then scatter the resulting salad over the risotto, along with the Parmesan shavings.

WARM CORNBREAD WITH MELTED BUTTER

This cornbread is rich, sunset yellow and full of sweetcorn flavour. It is a delicious mix of sweet and savoury, with a crisp outer crust and moist crumb within. This recipe uses the same instant polenta as on page 32, and most — if not all — of the other ingredients needed are common storecupboard items. As with nearly all baked goods, it is best while still warm from the oven, but it keeps well and reheats brilliantly in the microwave. Don't raise your eyebrows: microwaving cornbread — or sponge cakes or puddings for that matter — to warm them through causes them to steam slightly, which actually helps to keeps them moist. Make sure the butter is warm, like the cornbread.

Serves 8

125g unsalted butter, melted, plus more for the tin, pan or dish

340g can of sweetcorn

225g plain flour, sifted

225g instant polenta

10g baking powder

50g caster sugar

10g fine sea salt

pinch of chilli powder

250g whole milk

2 eggs, lightly beaten

60g clear honey

melted salted butter, to serve

~ Preheat the oven to 170°C. Butter a 26cm cake tin, ovenproof frying pan or gratin dish.

~ Drain the can of sweetcorn over a bowl, saving the liquid. Blend half the sweetcorn to a purée with all the liquid from the can, reserving the other half of the corn as kernels.

~ Sift together the flour, polenta, baking powder, sugar, salt and chilli powder in a large bowl.

~ Whisk together the milk, eggs, melted unsalted butter and clear honey in a separate bowl.

~ Add the liquid ingredients to the dry and whisk until smooth, then mix in both the corn purée and corn kernels.

~ Pour the batter into the prepared tin, pan or dish and bake immediately for 45 minutes, or until a toothpick inserted into the centre comes out clean and the edges start to separate from the pan. (Cooking time is quite long due to the moistness of the mix.)

~ Leave to cool for 10 minutes, then turn out on to a wire cooling rack.

~ Cut into pieces and serve with a healthy amount of melted butter on the side, to dip into or pour over.

WET POLENTA WITH PARMESAN & EGG YOLK

32

Warm, wet polenta, laden with dairy and aged Parmesan, is an undeniable crowd pleaser. It is rich and full of calories, but that is obviously why it tastes so good! Instant polenta cooks quickly and there is minimal preparation time. The ratio here of liquid to grain works perfectly. The egg yolk may well be gilding the lily, but sometimes more is more. Wet polenta works well as a substitute for mashed potato, served with braises and winter greens.

POLENTA

500g whole milk

1 teaspoon fine sea salt

8 strokes of finely grated nutmeg

100g instant polenta

50g mascarpone

50g unsalted butter, chopped

50g Parmesan cheese, finely grated

ASSEMBLE

4 egg yolks

black pepper

sea salt flakes

POLENTA

~ Bring the milk to the boil in a saucepan, then add the salt, nutmeg and polenta.

~ Bring to a simmer, whisking constantly, then cook for about 2 minutes until cooked and thickened.

~ Add the mascarpone, followed by the butter and Parmesan, whisking to melt.

ASSEMBLE

~ Spoon the polenta into warmed serving bowls and top each with an egg yolk.

~ Grind some black pepper on top and season the yolks with sea salt flakes.

EINKORN WHEAT PILAF

Einkorn wheat is an ancient grain, originally from Turkey. It is becoming more popular, largely due to its pleasing chewiness, so it is increasingly available. Here it is turned into a spiced pilaf with North African flavours, delicious with merguez sausages and tomato chutney. Leftovers are also great eaten cold.

Serves 8

RAISINS

1 jasmine teabag

60g golden raisins

PILAF

50g argan oil

1 red onion, sliced

4 celery sticks, cut 1cm thick on an angle

2 garlic cloves, crushed

250g einkorn wheat

1 cinnamon stick

150ml white vermouth

600ml water, or chicken stock

1 teaspoon fine sea salt

pinch of crushed black pepper

2 tablespoons chopped parsley leaves

1 tablespoon chopped dill

30 red grapes, halved

60g shelled unsalted pistachios, toasted (see page 19)

finely grated zest and juice of ½ lemon

RAISINS

~ Make a cup of tea with the jasmine teabag and add the raisins.

~ Leave to plump up – keeping the teabag in – for a couple of hours, or overnight.

PILAF

~ Preheat the oven to 180°C.

~ Heat the argan oil in an ovenproof and flameproof dish, then add the red onion and celery.

~ Season lightly with a pinch of salt and sweat for 5 minutes under a lid.

~ Add the garlic, wheat and cinnamon and stir to coat.

~ Pour in the vermouth and boil to reduce by half, then add the water or stock, salt and pepper and return to the boil. Cover and place in the oven.

~ Bake for 8 minutes, then remove the lid and cook for another 10 minutes.

~ Remove from the oven and check it is cooked. Also check the seasoning.

~ Fork lightly, adding the drained raisins, parsley, dill, grapes, pistachios and lemon zest and juice.

~ Leave to cool slightly before serving, as this is best enjoyed warm rather than hot.

BROWN RICE PUDDING, HONEY, DRIED FRUIT & CINNAMON

This twist on a rice pudding has real depth of flavour, from both the length of cooking time and the rich flavours within. Brown rice takes a long time to cook, but the preparation couldn't be any simpler. The nuttiness of the grain marries perfectly with the spices and honey, while the Greek yogurt, orange zest and Brazil nuts are a delicious foil for its richness.

This is a great example of what home cooking should be about: a fantastic end result with not much effort, accessible ingredients, and just the one pan to wash up at the end!

RICE PUDDING

1 litre whole milk

2 tablespoons soft brown sugar

2 tablespoons clear honey

100g brown basmati rice, soaked overnight in water, then drained

1 cinnamon stick

¼ teaspoon ground allspice

2 cloves

25g salted butter, chopped

12 dried apricots, halved

3 tablespoons golden raisins

ASSEMBLE

4 tablespoons Brazil nuts

finely grated zest of 1 orange

4 tablespoons thick Greek yogurt

RICE PUDDING

~ Preheat the oven to 160°C.

~ Mix all the ingredients together in a gratin dish or roasting tray and cover with foil.

~ Bake for 90 minutes, then remove the foil and stir.

~ Return to the oven without the foil and bake for another 30 minutes, or until tender. A nice skin will have developed, but the pudding should still be very moist.

~ Remove the pudding from the oven and leave to cool for 15 minutes.

ASSEMBLE

~ For the last 10 minutes that the pudding is cooking, spread the Brazil nuts on a baking sheet and toast them in the oven alongside the pudding. Remove the nuts from the oven and roughly chop them.

~ Grate the orange zest over the pudding and scatter over the nuts.

~ Spoon the pudding into warmed bowls, then top with a dollop of Greek yogurt, or serve it on the side.

DAIRY & EGGS

40

Dairy and eggs provide unparalleled vehicles for flavour. Their fat content gives length on the palate to anything to which they are added, causing flavours to linger as the dairy fat coats the tiny protrusions (*cilia*) of your taste buds.

This fat can be infused with many different flavourings to create a multi-layered sauce; the taste equivalent of a wall of sound. When you roast a chicken, you might add bacon lardons, thyme and garlic, a glug of wine, then – vitally – a splash of cream: all the other flavours will be carried by the cream. This is why dairy and eggs are so good with truffles, as both prolong the experience, allowing all those astounding aromas time to rise up through your palate and olfactory system and create an almost three-dimensional effect.

In Britain, we should take huge pride in our amazing dairy farmers and we have a duty to support them. We enjoy fantastic weather in this country for growing green grass, which is one reason why we are traditionally a dairy producing and eating country.

In the western world, we are all eating less dairy, as nut- and cereal-based substitutes become more popular. (Ironically, this has happened in tandem with an increase in home deliveries from the milkman, as home cooks look to use less plastic.) As a diner, I love cheese, eggs and cream and, as a chef, I find

it hard to imagine life without them. They are the cornerstone to so many preparations, especially to the enjoyment of simple home cooking.

And I admit that you need to enjoy dairy in moderation, so I recommend eating it less often but, when you do have it, to find the best. The best ice cream. The best cream. Free-range eggs with brilliant orange yolks. I use butter quite sparingly and only when I want you to taste it. In French cooking, you almost always start a dish by sautéing onions in butter, for instance, but I think that if you put butter in everything then you soon stop noticing it. I'm more likely to steam onions, for instance, to tease out their sweetness without any caramelisation, or to bake carrots whole wrapped in foil for a clean flavour. I like to cook in a way that preserves the authentic, *essential* flavours of the ingredients I use.

But, when you do cook with dairy, I urge you to use lots of it and enjoy it. When I do choose salted butter to sauté aromatics at the start of a dish – such as in the baked eggs recipe in this chapter – I know it will help to imbue the dish with seasoning from the very beginning. Seasoning is something you shouldn't notice as you eat; a dish should never taste salty, just delicious.

Sourcing the very best dairy will make a huge difference to your food. At my restaurant, our milk comes direct from the producer in Somerset. If you pour it into a glass next to a regular supermarket milk and compare the two, you can see a clear difference between them: the Somerset milk is decidedly yellow in colour, emanating from the grass fed to the cattle, and has a far better, richer flavour. The Spenwood cheese used in the dumplings in this chapter is from a village-based dairy. It's a hard sheep's cheese with lovely depth: a little bit nutty, a little bit sweet, a little bit tangy. It's refined enough to bracket with the likes of some of the European great cheeses such as Comté and Coolea: lovely to cook with and lovely to eat.

The majority of recipes in this chapter are winter warmers, rich concoctions that are hearty and comforting. This is somewhat inevitable, as we all crave dairy more when our bodies need its fat to help protect us from the cold. Tartiflette is a prime example, a dish traditionally served on frosty ski slopes. Cauliflower cheese is a classic due for a comeback, while a properly made croque monsieur is a thing of beauty. My baked eggs are a heartier version of shakshuka, while the ricotta dumplings are a very much lighter version of gnocchi (and far quicker to make, too).

You may wonder why I've bothered to give a scrambled egg recipe here. That's simple: it's something that almost everyone makes and in exactly the same way every time, because that's the way in which they have always made it without really knowing why. Hopefully my version will help you to make the very best scrambled eggs; a little understanding of *why* we do things is just as important as knowing *how* to do them.

SCRAMBLED EGGS ON TOAST

42

This may seem unexciting, but as it is a dish that most of us cook regularly, why not make it notably delicious every time? It may well be that the way you make scrambled eggs is born out of habit rather than culinary common sense.

There are a few key things to do to get this dish right. Serve it with big doorstops of brioche, to soak up the egg and provide that luxurious pillowy mouthfeel that a thin slice of granary bread just doesn't provide.

Have the eggs at room temperature before cooking, so they scramble evenly.

When starting the dish, get the butter slightly hotter than you may expect, so you get a ruffled, light scramble as the eggs cook and coagulate. Done this way, there should be strands of cooked egg, almost like stracciatella. Then reduce the heat and keep working the egg with a spatula so it doesn't stick. Don't use a whisk or you will break up those velvety strands of egg and have a more fragmented end result.

By adding cream at the end, you are helping to arrest the cooking process so the eggs stay loose.

As a general guide, cook the eggs for less time than you think; they should be quite wet and only just able to support their own weight.

Use the freshest eggs available. A fresh egg, when cracked on a plate, has a definite outline to the albumen and stays quite tight, whereas an older egg will spread out and have a watery, less viscous appearance.

EGGS

12 eggs, at room temperature

70g salted butter

2 pinches of fine sea salt

140g whipping cream

ASSEMBLE

brioche loaf

salted butter, softened

––––

EGGS

~ Whisk the eggs in a bowl.

~ Heat the butter in a wide pan over a medium heat until just sizzling and hot, but not starting to colour.

~ Add the eggs. Leave for 10 seconds, then, using a spatula, beat regularly but gently over a low heat until the eggs are fluffy and barely set, adding the salt.

~ Remove from the heat and add the cream to arrest the cooking, mixing it in without breaking up the ruffles of egg too much. Check the seasoning.

ASSEMBLE

~ Meanwhile, preheat a grill to high. Slice 4 x 3cm-thick slices of brioche and grill on both sides until light golden. Butter lightly.

~ Top the buttered toasts with the eggs.

CROQUE MONSIEUR

The best ideas and most refined recipes are invariably the simplest, but simplicity can be hard to do well. It is frustrating if a recipe that looks easy on the page doesn't come out as you want it to, but that may be only because you don't know what you are doing wrong. A croque monsieur is a great example of how layers of attention to detail, thought and consideration can transform something from an everyday snack into an entirely more sophisticated dish.

This is best served with a salad of shredded celeriac dressed with a classic vinaigrette and crème fraîche (see page 205 for a similar celeriac concoction).

If you want to push the boat out, croque monsieur is also delicious with a layer of black truffle shavings running through the middle and scattered on top.

GARLIC TRUFFLE BUTTER

125g salted butter, softened

1 garlic clove, crushed

1 teaspoon black truffle oil (optional)

BECHAMEL

500g whole milk

2 cloves

pinch of ground mace

pinch of freshly grated nutmeg

50g unsalted butter

40g plain flour

125g Gruyère cheese, grated

1 teaspoon Dijon mustard

1 teaspoon black truffle oil (optional)

4 egg yolks

fine sea salt

ASSEMBLE

white bloomer loaf

Dijon mustard

Gruyère cheese, coarsely grated

8 thin-cut slices of good-quality sandwich ham

GARLIC TRUFFLE BUTTER

~ Mix all the ingredients together to combine evenly. Keep the flavoured butter at room temperature.

BECHAMEL

~ Bring the milk to the boil in a saucepan, then remove from the heat, add the spices and allow to infuse for 15 minutes. Strain.

~ Melt the butter in a saucepan over a gentle heat and add the flour, whisking to combine. Add the infused milk gradually, whisking until smooth. Bring to the boil, again whisking constantly, until thickened.

~ Remove from the heat and whisk in the remaining ingredients with a pinch of fine sea salt.

ASSEMBLE

~ Preheat the oven to 180°C and also heat the grill to high.

~ Cut the bread across into slices no thicker than 1cm, to give 8 slices.

~ Spread one side of each slice generously with garlic truffle butter and toast under the grill until golden all over (don't turn it, you want it to toast on just one side).

~ Lay 4 of the bread slices, toasted sides down, on a baking tray lined with baking parchment (these will be the bases of the sandwiches), spread lightly with Dijon mustard, then top generously with grated cheese. Lay over 2 slices of the ham and finally more cheese.

~ Top with the remaining toasted bread slices, this time toasted sides up.

~ Spread the tops neatly with the bechamel, then glaze under the hot grill until golden.

~ Place in the oven for 5 minutes, until the cheese has melted in the middle and the croques are warm throughout. Cut in half, if you like, and serve straightaway.

BAKED EGGS WITH TOMATO, BUTTER BEANS & PAPRIKA

A gentler version of shakshuka. Whereas that is punchy, this is much more a warm embrace. It's a one-pan wonder, but do try to find a large wide pan or dish for this. There are very few occasions when I would serve tomatoes with butter and cream rather than olive oil, but here it does work better to soften the intense sweet-sour flavours of the tomato fondue, making them more refined. Not one for the purists, but there is room for everyone!

This is delicious with a spoonful of hung yogurt (see page 294) melting over the top.

60g salted butter

1 red onion, finely sliced

1 red pepper, finely chopped

4 garlic cloves, crushed

1 heaped teaspoon sweet paprika

1 level teaspoon cumin seeds

pinch of chilli flakes

1 cinnamon stick

400g can of tomatoes, crushed

4 ripe fresh tomatoes, cored and roughly chopped

2 teaspoons caster sugar

2 tablespoons sherry vinegar

150g double cream

400g can of butter beans, drained and rinsed

4 handfuls of spinach (leaf or baby)

4 eggs

8 turns of crushed black pepper

4 tablespoons roughly chopped coriander leaves and stems

fine sea salt

thick Greek yogurt, to serve

———

~ Preheat the oven to 180°C.

~ Heat the butter in a large, wide ovenproof saucepan, or flameproof oven dish, over a medium heat and add the onion; season lightly with salt.

~ Cook until light golden, then add the pepper, season lightly again and cook for another 5 minutes, still over a medium heat.

~ Add the garlic and spices and cook for another couple of minutes.

~ Add the canned and fresh tomatoes, season lightly and add the sugar, vinegar and cream.

~ Simmer for about 30 minutes, then mix in the butter beans and spinach and cook for another couple of minutes, just to wilt the leaves.

~ Make 4 dimples in the sauce and break in the eggs. Season them lightly with salt and black pepper, then bake for about 10 minutes until they're just set.

~ Leave to cool for 15 minutes: this is infinitely more satisfying when warm rather than piping hot. Sprinkle with coriander and serve, with the yogurt.

CAULIFLOWER CHEESE WITH BERKSWELL & VINTAGE CHEDDAR

A forgotten delight. Our collective memory of this dish is often tainted by the unwelcome spectre of school food — that is, overcooked and watery — but properly cooked cauliflower cheese, using good-quality cheese and cooking the cauliflower only until al dente (rather than to death), is absolutely delicious. It makes a great accompaniment to sausages or pork chops, but it is equally worthy as a meal in itself, with a green salad. Feel free to swap the cheeses. Ogleshield and Spenwood would also work brilliantly together, as would Taleggio and Dolcelatte, if you wanted something both sharper and more Italian.

1 large or 2 small cauliflowers

600g whole milk

2 cloves

6 strokes of nutmeg

pinch of ground mace

pinch of cayenne pepper

1 teaspoon Dijon mustard

50g salted butter

40g plain flour

80g Berkswell cheese, grated

80g vintage Cheddar cheese, grated

fine sea salt

51

~ Cut the cauliflower into quarters and blanch in boiling salted water (allow 20g salt for each 1 litre of water) for 6 minutes for a large cauliflower, or 4 minutes for smaller cauliflowers.

~ Refresh in iced water, then drain well and place on a tray lined with a new J-cloth to dry.

~ Bring the milk to the boil, then add the spices and mustard, remove from the heat and set aside to infuse for 30 minutes. Pass through a sieve.

~ Melt the butter in a saucepan and whisk in the flour to form a roux; it should thicken, bubble and turn light golden. Add the hot milk gradually, whisking well after each addition, to make a smooth sauce. Ensure it comes to the boil, to cook out the flour.

~ Remove from the heat and add both types of cheese, whisking to melt. Cool to room temperature.

~ Preheat the oven to 190°C.

~ Place the cauliflower pieces in an ovenproof dish that fits them snugly in a single layer, cut-side down, then pour over the cheese sauce.

~ Place in the oven for 20 minutes; if you want a bit more colour after this time, place under a preheated grill until browned and bubbling. Leave at room temperature for 10 minutes to cool slightly before serving.

RICOTTA DUMPLINGS

This recipe contains just about every iteration of dairy. The dumplings are essentially a gnudi: a variation of gnocchi, but far lighter and less starchy due to the use of ricotta in place of potato. Here, they have been anglicised by the addition of Spenwood, a delicious sheep's milk cheese. It has a nutty caramel edge and just a slight tang from the ewe's milk. I love cooking with it.

The dumplings are very easy to prepare, and are also fantastic just served with a sage butter, or fresh peas and Parmesan. This version is heavier winter comfort food, served with a rich Spenwood and rosemary cream. The hazelnut oil and lemon thyme are a delicious addition, but also optional; feel free to omit or substitute as you wish.

SPENWOOD CREAM

400g double cream

50g whole milk

100g salted butter

1 teaspoon black truffle oil (optional)

120g Spenwood cheese, finely grated

2 rosemary sprigs, bruised

1 garlic clove, finely sliced

pinch of fine sea salt

DUMPLINGS

400g creamy ricotta

200g Spenwood cheese, finely grated

125g plain flour, plus more to dust

1 egg, plus 1 egg yolk

1 teaspoon fine sea salt

¼ teaspoon ground mace

ASSEMBLE

4 handfuls of kale, coarse stems removed, leaves ripped into small pieces and washed

4 handfuls of mixed wild mushrooms, briefly washed (see page 80)

200g can of cooked chestnuts, reserving 8 for presentation

4 tablespoons hazelnut oil (optional)

4 tablespoons lemon thyme leaves (optional)

SPENWOOD CREAM

- Bring the cream, milk and butter to the boil in a saucepan, then remove from the heat and add the truffle oil and salt.
- Blend in the Spenwood cheese using a stick blender, then stir in the rosemary and garlic.
- Infuse for 5 minutes, then pass through a sieve into a wide saucepan.

DUMPLINGS

- Mix everything together in a food mixer and beat until smooth.
- Pinch off small pieces, each around 15g, and roll into neat balls between your palms. Keep on a lightly floured tray.
- Bring a pan of salted water to a simmer (using 10g salt for each 1 litre water) and add the dumplings. They will rise to the surface once cooked. Simmer gently for 5 minutes, then drain.

ASSEMBLE

- Blanch the kale in boiling salted water (again using 10g salt for each 1 litre water) for 4 minutes, then drain the leaves very well.
- Transfer the drained dumplings into the pan of Spenwood cream.
- Add the mushrooms, kale and chestnuts and heat to soften the mushrooms; this should only take 2–3 minutes over a medium heat.
- Divide between 4 warmed serving bowls, drizzle over the hazelnut oil and scatter with the lemon thyme, if using, then grate over the reserved chestnuts.

TARTIFLETTE

56

A French mountain dish of potatoes with bacon, onions, cream and a whole Reblochon cheese. This is probably your recommended weekly calorific intake in a single bowl, but it is the sort of dish you eat just once a year. And well worth it. Maybe plan a long walk for afterwards, or beforehand, to build up an appetite. Actually, definitely have the walk first as, realistically, you'll be asleep within minutes of your last mouthful. Reblochon is a washed rind cheese, and you need that pungency to cut through the bacon and the cream. No need to peel the potatoes, as the skins add taste and texture here. This is most definitely a meal in itself; serve with a crisp green salad in a sharp mustardy dressing.

1kg Charlotte potatoes, scrubbed but unpeeled, sliced 1cm thick

1 teaspoon fine sea salt

200g Alsace bacon, or pancetta, or smoked streaky bacon, chopped into 1cm lardons

30g salted butter

2 white onions, sliced

250g white wine

300g double cream

2 garlic cloves, crushed, plus 1 garlic clove, halved

1 Reblochon cheese

~ Season the potatoes evenly with the salt, then place in a single layer in a steamer basket.

~ Steam over a pan of boiling water for 20 minutes until just cooked through.

~ In this time, colour the lardons in the butter until golden and the bacon fat has rendered. Strain through a sieve, reserving the fat.

~ Return the fat to the pan and add the onions, season lightly with salt and fry until light golden: about 5 minutes.

~ Return the bacon to the pan, then pour in the wine.

~ Bring to the boil, then add the cream and boil for 2 minutes. Remove from the heat and add the crushed garlic, followed by the steamed potatoes. Leave to cool to room temperature.

~ Preheat the oven to 180°C.

~ Meanwhile, cut the cheese. First, cut a thin round from the top of the whole cheese, about one-third of its total depth. Slice the rest into 1cm slices.

~ Rub a round ovenproof dish with the halved garlic clove, then spoon in a layer of potatoes, followed by a layer of cheese. Repeat twice more, finishing with the cheese disc on top.

~ Cover with foil and bake for 30 minutes, then glaze under a preheated grill until golden and bubbling. Serve.

VEGETAB

LES

60

A decade ago, while I was struggling to raise funds to open my first restaurant, I wrote to a few large restaurant groups to try to find a head chef position, but one in which I could cook my own dishes. More than one potential employer told me that my proferred menus contained too many vegetables. Thankfully, I doubt the same would happen today. (And no, I wasn't offered a job!) Vegetables are no longer just a token garnish, a side dish, something you feel you have to eat under duress or social pressure.

We live in interesting times. Human beings are biologically omnivorous, but I wonder if we are at the start of a change and if, over the coming millennia, our dental and digestive functions might evolve to become more like that of herbivores, as people either choose to stop eating so much meat, or less of it is available to us.

Certainly the trends are heading that way. Over the last few years, for many people, eating vegetable-centred food has become habit: an engrained choice. We don't want to feel bloated or lethargic after a meal, we want to feel satisfied but not satiated, and the diversity and seasonal variety of vegetables make it easy to incorporate them into a prime position in our diets, with one for each mood and every occasion. When we roast cauliflower, for instance, we don't just appreciate the nuttiness that the heat brings out in the flavour, but the roasted vegetable's texture – that mix of dense flesh and tenderness – which is near-carnal in its appeal.

Many of the recipes in this chapter celebrate a single vegetable – Carrot Tartare, Cauliflower Couscous or Ripe Tomato on Toast, to name but three – and that element of showcasing one ingredient encapsulates my style of cooking. It is also essentially the role of a chef: to take the best ingredients and turn them into the finest versions of themselves. To do that, we need to question why we like a vegetable in the first place, and heighten that quality.

In the summer, we look forward to ripe tomatoes – the very best should be served raw to show off their fragrance – crisp vegetable salads, roast aubergines and peppers. In the autumn and winter, there are slow-roast wedges of warm pumpkin, hot jacket potatoes with bitter leaves, root vegetables simmered until tender or baked until their natural sweetness comes out, rendering them comforting and yielding; dishes which are just exactly what we want to eat at this time of year when they are at their peak. And best of all, for most cooks, is spring time: we have the bounty of fresh peas, verdant broad beans and asparagus to play with, all at their most delicious when treated simply, cooked sympathetically and enlivened only with fresh herbs.

Vegetables, already adaptable, healthy and inexpensive, have become even more versatile through our ever-improving access to the global larder. Green beans can be turned into tempura, cauliflower roasted whole with *vadouvan* (a French colonial Indian-influenced spice mix), or aubergine painted with a paste of Japanese miso and honey.

It really is vital to respect vegetables when cooking them, especially when they are the main focus of a dish. Some benefit from just a quick burst of heat, while others need to be cooked low and slow to show at their best. Roots can be left in quite thick pieces, which adds an extra level of indulgence and comfort, akin to eating a chateaubriand rather than a minute steak. There are a good number of recipes in this chapter in which vegetables are simply dressed or lightly softened by the addition of salt or acidity, too, which preserves the majority of their nutrients.

Think about the water in a vegetable when you are cooking it, because certain vegetables welcome a lot of seasoning due to their water content; tomatoes and pumpkins, for instance, can take a heavy hand with the salt. But when you season a pan of spinach you need to visualise its cooked volume; you might be tempted to put in an amount of salt that reflects the quantity of raw leaves, but if you do that the result will be too salty.

Serving vegetables at the correct temperature is also important. Tomatoes must be at room temperature, as must avocados, because of their high fat content; if you serve them straight from the refrigerator they will be too firm. Just a little bit of thought and consideration is needed, but none of it is complicated.

Vegetable cookery has a pleasure all of its own, and in spirit is very much a celebration of nature. You will find that you return to these recipes not because, nutritionally speaking, you feel you should, but because you crave them.

CAULIFLOWER COUSCOUS

A great vegetarian dish that is moreish, full of nutrients and can be prepared in minutes. Feel free to add different dried fruits, spices, herbs or nuts: whatever you have in your cupboards will be just fine... Figs, basil, apricots or coriander would all be most welcome here.

This is great with barbecued meat and fish, especially if it has Middle Eastern flavours.

COUSCOUS

1 jasmine teabag

30g sultanas

250g cauliflower, chopped

5 tablespoons mixed nuts and seeds: pine nuts, pistachios or poppy seeds

1 tablespoon chopped dill

1 tablespoon chopped lovage or parsley leaves

1 tablespoon chopped mint leaves

30g olive oil

finely grated zest and juice of ½ lemon

seeds of 1 pomegranate

40g red grapes, halved

½ garlic clove, minced

fine sea salt

ASSEMBLE

Sesame labneh (see page 294)

Dukkah (see page 294)

COUSCOUS

~ Make a cup of tea with the jasmine teabag and add the sultanas. Leave to soak for a couple of hours ideally, though at least while you prepare the other ingredients.

~ Blend the cauliflower in a food processor until the texture resembles couscous. Transfer to a mixing bowl and season lightly with salt.

~ Toast the nuts and seeds in a hot dry pan – or in an oven preheated to 180°C – until golden, season lightly with salt, then add to the cauliflower along with the herbs, olive oil, lemon zest and juice, pomegranate seeds, grapes, garlic and drained sultanas.

~ Keep at room temperature until serving, as that's a far more enjoyable way to eat this than when it's straight out of the refrigerator.

ASSEMBLE

~ Serve the couscous in a bowl with the labneh on the side, topped with a generous scattering of dukkah.

GRILLED SHIITAKE, DANDELION & PANCETTA

This dressing can be used on anything from grilled scallops to jacket potatoes... smoked bacon makes most things taste better. The leftover bacon can be sprinkled over future suppers. Wilting the pancetta just to soften it renders the texture silky, and is much more luxurious than cooking it to a crisp.

SMOKED BACON DRESSING

250g smoked streaky bacon

250g vegetable oil

juice of ½ lemon

2 tablespoons Chardonnay vinegar

1 garlic clove, crushed

4 egg yolks

1 teaspoon Dijon mustard

sea salt flakes

SHIITAKE

500g shiitake mushrooms

75g olive oil

1 garlic clove, crushed

PANCETTA

12 rashers of pancetta

ASSEMBLE

4 handfuls of dandelion, or other bitter leaves

8 tarragon sprigs, leaves stripped

8 lemon thyme sprigs, leaves stripped

SMOKED BACON DRESSING

~ Chop the bacon into 2cm slices and place in a pan with the vegetable oil.

~ Bring to 130°C (gently bubbling), then reduce the heat to its lowest and cook until the bacon is golden brown. Leave to cool, then strain through a sieve into a bowl to obtain a rich bacon fat.

~ Blend the remaining ingredients with 70g water. Gradually add the bacon fat to emulsify into a creamy dressing.

SHIITAKE

~ Preheat the grill to its hottest setting.

~ Toss the mushrooms, olive oil and garlic with a generous pinch of salt and scatter on a baking tray in one layer.

~ Grill aggressively until golden brown.

PANCETTA

~ Lay the pancetta on a baking tray.

~ Grill until just wilted and only lightly crisped in parts (this can be as quick as 30 seconds, so keep an eye on it).

ASSEMBLE

~ Drizzle some smoked bacon dressing all around 4 plates, then scatter over the mushrooms and pancetta.

~ Toss the dandelion leaves lightly in the bacon dressing and scatter over, with the tarragon and lemon thyme.

ICED WATERMELON GAZPACHO

This — perhaps my favourite chilled summer soup — can be served plain, or turned into a quick summer lunch with some feta cheese, basil leaves and toasted pumpkins seeds. Here it is passed through a sieve so it is smooth, but you can keep it chunky if you prefer. If watermelon isn't available, use any other ripe melon. A small amount of green pepper here gives the gazpacho its distinguishing grassiness. When I use both white wine vinegar and Chardonnay vinegar in a recipe, it is for a good reason: white wine vinegar is much more acidic, while Chardonnay vinegar is fragrant and sweet. This must *be served ice cold.*

1kg ripe watermelon, peeled and chopped (or see recipe introduction)

180g cucumber, peeled and chopped

50g green pepper, deseeded and chopped

30g shallot, roughly chopped

½ garlic clove, roughly chopped

1 tablespoon white wine vinegar

2 tablespoons Chardonnay vinegar

juice of ¼ lemon

pinch of chilli flakes

2 teaspoons fine sea salt

4 lemon verbena sprigs, bruised, or 2 lemon grass stalks, trimmed, bruised and finely chopped

4 teaspoons olive oil

~ Mix everything together except the lemon verbena or lemon grass and olive oil. Cover with cling film and leave for 4 hours in the refrigerator.

~ Blitz in a blender, in batches if necessary, for just 5 seconds each time, to a rough purée.

~ Pass through a sieve twice: the first time pushing the mixture through with the back of a spoon, the second time just tapping the sieve.

~ Add the lemon verbena or lemon grass and leave in the freezer, along with 4 serving cups or bowls, for 30 minutes, or until ice-cold.

~ Strain the herbs from the soup, then pour it into the frosted cups or bowls and drizzle each with a little olive oil.

~ Serve immediately.

CARROT TARTARE WITH SUNFLOWER SEEDS, MUSTARD & TARRAGON

A tartare is traditionally made with fish or meat and served raw. This is neither! It just feels apt to call it a tartare, as I always think of a 'tartare' as a hero ingredient which is chopped, then mixed with seasonings that elevate it. I hope the name will also give a fresh perspective. You may read this recipe and decide you want to make a tartare with celeriac, hazelnuts and pear, for example.

If you find carrots with their green tops, do buy them, as they taste more of carrots than the roots themselves. If you make extra, enjoy it the next day with toasted pitta.

6 carrots, peeled and grated
(600g prepared weight)

75g virgin rapeseed oil

15g clear honey

8 tablespoons sunflower seeds,
plus more to serve

1 orange

1 tablespoon wholegrain mustard,
or to taste

2 tablespoons roughly chopped tarragon
leaves, or to taste, plus more to serve

2 tablespoons chopped carrot tops, if
available, or to taste, plus more to serve

4 tablespoons white wine vinegar,
or to taste

300g thick Greek yogurt

fine sea salt

sunflower petals (optional), to serve

~ Mix the carrots, oil, honey and a pinch of salt in a bowl. If you have a microwave, cover and cook for 3 minutes at 700W (the high setting) until just tender. Or preheat the oven to 170°C, wrap the mixture in foil and bake for 20 minutes. Leave to cool.

~ Preheat the oven to 170°C if you didn't do so before, then place the sunflower seeds on a baking tray and toast for 10 minutes, or until golden brown.

~ Finely grate the orange zest into a small bowl. To segment the orange, cut a thin slice from the top and bottom so you can see a wheel of flesh. Placing it on one end, run a knife down the fruit in a curved shape, following its contours, to remove all the white pith with the skin. Using a small, sharp knife, cut between the membranes, working over a bowl to catch all the juice. The segments will fall into the bowl. Chop them into small pieces.

~ Place the carrots on a chopping board and run through them with a large knife to create the consistency of a tartare. It should be almost like minced meat, but with a bit more identity.

~ Mix in the remaining ingredients, add a pinch of salt and check the seasoning. If you want more salt or vinegar, herbs or mustard, adjust accordingly.

~ Scatter with tarragon, carrot tops, petals, if using, and sunflower seeds.

69

RIPE TOMATO
ON TOAST

The key here is in contrasts: crisp toasts with fleshy tomato; smoky grilled bread next to the sweetness of what lies on top. Ciabatta is fine to use, but if you can find pan cristal *from a Spanish store, get it, as it makes incomparably crisp toast. Buy the best tomatoes you can find in advance of when you need them, so you can ripen them at room temperature. (Scientific studies show a marked decrease in flavour upon refrigeration.) Finally, marinate them in a single layer to ensure the seasoning is evenly applied. It is really important with something this simple to do it perfectly.*

TOMATOES

1 garlic clove, peeled, halved and dipped in fine sea salt

2 large, ripe *coeur de boeuf* tomatoes

3 tablespoons white balsamic vinegar

1 teaspoon fine sea salt

1 teaspoon caster sugar

3 tablespoons extra virgin olive oil

6 basil sprigs

3 rosemary sprigs

ASSEMBLE

8 thin slices of ciabatta (5mm thick, ideally) or *pan cristal*

4 tablespoons extra virgin olive oil

24 basil leaves

12 pitted black olives, washed and halved

TOMATOES

- Rub the split and salted clove of garlic all over the platter or roasting tray that you will use to marinate the tomatoes. Reserve this garlic for later.

- Slice the tomatoes with a sharp serrated knife to just under 1cm thick and place the slices in a single layer on a large baking tray or platter.

- For the dressing, blend the vinegar, salt, sugar and oil together, then spoon or brush it over the tomatoes generously, slice by slice.

- Bruise the basil and rosemary by rubbing the sprigs vigorously between your palms, then distribute them evenly on top of the tomato slices.

- Leave at room temperature for 1 hour, then baste with their juices.

- Leave for another hour, then repeat the basting and remove the aromatic herbs, which will have wilted.

ASSEMBLE

- Grill the ciabatta on both sides in a hot chargrill pan until lightly charred, then drizzle with olive oil and rub with the cut side of the reserved garlic.

- Drizzle generously with the remaining oil and top each slice with a basil leaf.

- Top with the tomato slices to cover the surface of the bread, adding basil leaves and olives.

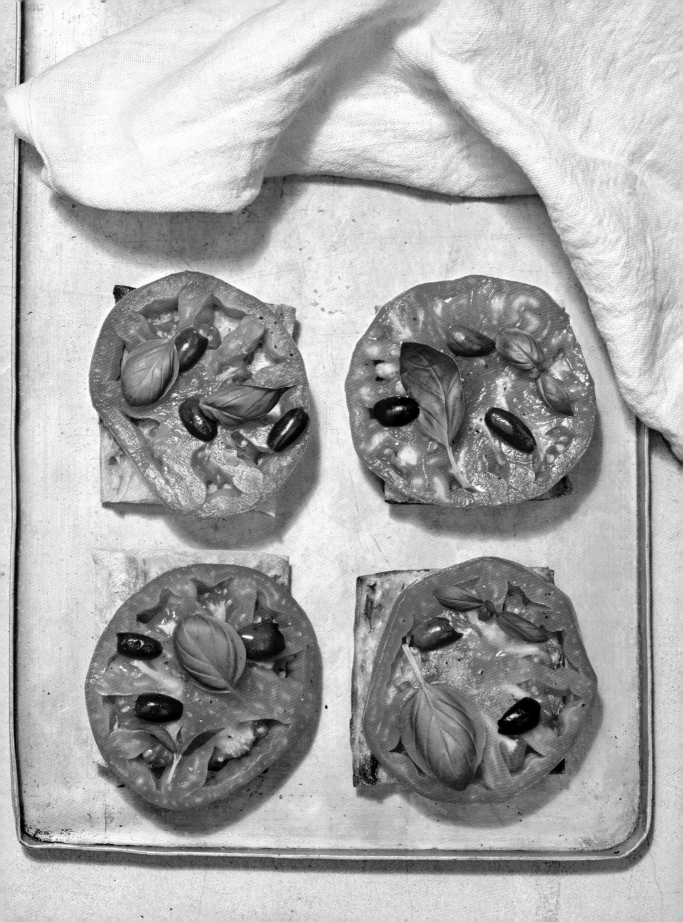

BAKED AUTUMN VEGETABLES; WARM CHESTNUT BROTH

72

This is a great example of minimal ingredients combining with minimal effort for maximum reward. Baking in foil packages traps all the steam and flavours, so the vegetables remain moist. Just cut the vegetables that take longest to cook into smaller pieces. The lemon thyme shines through the broth and vegetables, and by adding it at the end, you keep its spritely flavour. There's no need to peel the vegetables, as the roasted skins have a delicious nuttiness.

VEGETABLES

150g salted butter

1 garlic clove, crushed

⅛ nutmeg, finely grated

1kg vegetables, such as carrots, beetroot, parsnips, Hispi cabbage, Jerusalem artichokes and pumpkin, cut into pieces

pinch of fine sea salt

BROTH

350g cooked chestnuts

800g whole milk

50g unsalted butter

20g muscovado sugar

20g molasses

12g fine sea salt

ASSEMBLE

4 teaspoons lemon thyme leaves

VEGETABLES

~ Preheat the oven to 180°C.

~ Warm the butter in a pan and add the garlic and nutmeg.

~ Take a roll of foil and tear a length over a roasting tray so it extends well over the sides. Repeat in the other direction to make a cross.

~ Scatter the vegetables on in a single layer, season lightly with salt, then drizzle over the garlic butter.

~ Bring in the foil ends and seal to make a package, then place in the oven.

~ Cook the vegetables until tender but still holding their shape, 1–1¼ hours. Anything less than soft, and the full potential of their sweetness will not be achieved. Test with the tip of a knife.

BROTH

~ Bring everything to a simmer with 600g water and cook for 5 minutes. Blend until smooth.

ASSEMBLE

~ Divide the vegetables between 4 warmed bowls and drizzle over their cooking juices from the foil package.

~ Scatter over the lemon thyme, allowing a full teaspoon per person, then pour over the warm broth.

CRISP COLESLAW
WITH CARAWAY

Forget the disgusting supermarket fodder, devoid of nutrients, texture and taste. This coleslaw is vibrant, crisp and delicious, it actually tastes healthy. A welcome level of acidity comes from the lemon and vinegar, while a judicious amount of mayonnaise and sour cream ensures the vegetables are not drowned in fat or dairy content. Caraway seed has a strong medicinal taste and smell, not dissimilar to eucalyptus, but adds a clean burst of fragrance to the coleslaw that accentuates its crisp freshness.

Keeping the vegetables in long pieces when they are cut — rather than grated as is more usual — gives greater pleasure, as it imparts an almost noodle-like mouthfeel.

This is delicious on toasted pitta or served alongside anything fatty or cooked over charcoal: a great foil for big flavours.

200g white onion (ideally), or brown onion, halved and finely sliced

300g red cabbage, cored and shredded

200g carrots, shredded

200g celeriac, shredded

2 teaspoons fine sea salt

juice of 1 lemon

4 tablespoons Chardonnay vinegar

180g Mayonnaise (see page 294)

60g sour cream

40g wholegrain mustard, or to taste

3 teaspoons caraway seeds, toasted (see page 19), or to taste, plus a little more to serve

~ Combine the vegetables in a bowl and dress with the salt, lemon juice and vinegar. Mix well, cover and leave for 1 hour at room temperature; they will wilt lightly.

~ Mix the remaining ingredients in a separate bowl, then stir into the vegetables. Check the seasoning, acidity and pokiness, adjusting with mustard or caraway, if you like.

~ Serve in a bowl at room temperature or lightly chilled, topped with a scattering of caraway seeds.

BEETROOT HUMMUS, LOVAGE & SESAME FLATBREAD

A delicious, vibrant and healthy snack or light lunch. There is no point making any less than this amount of hummus, as it keeps for several days in the refrigerator and is a wonderful accompaniment to grilled meat and fish.

Nearly all cans of chickpeas are 400g, which gives just 250g drained weight, so this recipe will use up precisely one can. (I hate having a tiny amount of leftovers that you don't want to throw away but, at the same time, isn't really enough to make anything with, so I won't do that to you!)

If you can't get hold of white balsamic vinegar, then substitute Chardonnay vinegar or regular balsamic. When making these flatbreads, or any other bread for that matter, a good trick is to put the liquid in the mixing bowl first, then add the flour. This way, you aren't left with any unmixed dry ingredients at the end when you empty out the bowl.

If you're short on time, just buy some flatbreads rather than making your own.

HUMMUS

500g raw beetroot, washed

250g canned chickpeas (1 regular can), drained and rinsed

1 garlic clove, peeled

finely grated zest and juice of 1 lemon

30g tahini

2 tablespoons white balsamic vinegar

1 tablespoon ground cumin

75g olive oil

50g vegetable oil

½ tablespoon fine sea salt

FLATBREAD

8g fresh yeast (if possible), or 7g sachet fast-action dried yeast

400g strong white bread flour

100g semolina flour

12g caster sugar

12g fine sea salt

vegetable oil, for oiling

2 tablespoons black sesame seeds

2 tablespoons white sesame seeds

4 tablespoons olive oil

1 garlic clove, peeled and halved

pinch of sea salt flakes

4 tablespoons roughly chopped lovage leaves, or parsley leaves

HUMMUS

~ Place the beetroot in a large pan of cold water, deep enough to cover them entirely. Simmer for about 90 minutes until tender, then drain. Leave until warm enough to handle, then peel (wear plastic gloves if you prefer, as the juices stain). This should leave you with 400g cooked, peeled beetroot.

~ Roughly chop the beetroot into large chunks, then blend with the remaining ingredients to achieve a vibrant purple semi-smooth hummus. Check the seasoning, then place in a deep bowl.

FLATBREAD

~ Dissolve the yeast in 375g warm water (it should be at body temperature) and place in the bowl of a food mixer fitted with a dough hook.

~ Add both types of flour and the sugar and beat on low speed for 30 seconds just to combine. Leave to autolyse for 15 minutes: in this time, the flour will become fully hydrated, enabling greater gluten production and a superior dough.

~ Mix for 10 minutes, then finally mix in the salt. Adding the salt at the end helps protect it from attacking the yeast and impeding the rise.

~ Divide into 4, then roll into balls. Place on an oiled baking tray and top with an oiled sheet of cling film. Prove at room temperature for 1 hour.

~ Roll each piece out to about 1cm thick in slipper shapes.

~ Place both colours of sesame seeds, white and black, in a dry pan and toast over a high heat until the white seeds are golden. Season lightly with salt and transfer to a small bowl.

~ Heat a chargrill pan until very hot, then brush with olive oil.

~ Place a rolled-out flatbread on top and grill for 1 minute until puffed up and smoky. Turn over and repeat. Remove from the pan and keep warm while you cook the remaining flatbreads.

~ Drizzle them all generously with olive oil, then rub each on one side with the split garlic clove.

~ Sprinkle over the toasted sesame seeds, sea salt flakes and lovage.

TO SERVE

~ Serve on a large platter alongside the bowl of beetroot hummus.

WILD MUSHROOMS & FRIED DUCK EGG ON TOAST

Feel free to use morels, shiitake or plain old chestnut mushrooms for this recipe. There is no need for cream here; the richness comes from the butter and egg yolk. Duck eggs have a large, rich yolk, but hen's eggs would be fine, too. Pea shoots are fairly common as a salad leaf, but here they are wilted with the buttery mushrooms, lightening the concoction with their pleasant grassy burst. The parsley should just be roughly chopped, as you will notice it more. Finally: a note on fried eggs... Cook them gently over no more than a medium heat; there should be no colour on the underside.

MUSHROOMS

250g wild mushrooms

75g salted butter

1 garlic clove, crushed

juice of ⅛ lemon

2 tablespoons chopped parsley leaves

fine sea salt

ASSEMBLE

4 duck eggs

1 tablespoon salted butter

handful of pea shoots

handful of wild garlic leaves, if available

4 slices of wholemeal bread, toasted

sea salt flakes

black pepper

garlic or chive flowers, if available

MUSHROOMS

~ Fill a sink or large bowl with water and add the wild mushrooms. Agitate them lightly to help remove any grit or dirt, then leave for 5 minutes, remove with a slotted spoon and place on a tray well lined with kitchen paper. Leave to air dry, then slice, depending on size. A plate of food, no matter how delicious, is ruined by a trace of grit, so I prefer to wash mushrooms, albeit at a slight detriment to the flavour.

~ Heat the butter in a frying pan, add the mushrooms and garlic and salt lightly. Cover with a lid and cook until just wilted, 2–3 minutes.

~ Add the lemon juice and 4 tablespoons water and mix to make an emulsion with the butter, then remove from the heat and add the parsley.

ASSEMBLE

~ Fry the duck eggs gently in the salted butter in a separate frying pan, finishing them under a hot grill just to set the yolks, if needed. Season with sea salt flakes and black pepper.

~ Add the pea shoots and wild garlic, if using, to the mushrooms, just to wilt slightly for a few seconds.

~ Place the toasts on plates, then spoon over the mushroom juices, eggs, mushrooms and greens. Decorate with the garlic or chive flowers, if using.

PUMPKIN, GRACEBURN & BASIL FRITTERS

Graceburn is a favourite cheese of mine: it could be pigeon-holed as 'English feta', though it is made from cow's milk rather than ewe's. More velvety and less crumbly than feta, it adds tang and salinity in much the same way. This recipe can be modified to almost any vegetable-herb-cheese combination: try sliced onions with thyme and Gorgonzola, or grated courgette with mint and goat's cheese. The fritters can be rolled the day before, then fried to order; the dip needs to be made ahead.

DIP

300g Greek yogurt

30g virgin rapeseed oil, more to serve

2 teaspoons nigella or cumin seeds, toasted (see page 19), more to serve

6–7 basil leaves, more to serve

FRITTERS

1.2kg pumpkin (prepared weight), peeled and coarsely grated

10g fine sea salt, plus more to serve

60g spring onions, finely sliced

30g basil leaves, ripped or chopped

2 small eggs, lightly beaten

180g plain flour

200g Graceburn cheese, chopped into 1.5cm cubes

vegetable oil, for deep-frying

pinch of smoked paprika

DIP

~ Spoon the yogurt into a muslin-lined sieve placed over a bowl. Wrap the muslin over the top and chill overnight, until very thick.

~ Whisk everything together to combine and transfer to a bowl.

~ Scatter a few extra seeds, basil leaves and a drizzle of oil on top to serve.

FRITTERS

~ Season the grated pumpkin with the salt. Leave in a colander for 1 hour with a plate on top loaded with a can of something heavy to weigh it down.

~ Squeeze dry by hand, then place in a tea towel, roll up like a Christmas cracker and squeeze out all the water.

~ Transfer to a bowl and mix in all the remaining ingredients except the oil and smoked paprika, adding the cheese at the end so it doesn't crumble too much. Chill for about 1 hour, until firm enough to handle. Roll into balls of about 2 tablespoons each.

~ Prepare a deep saucepan with enough vegetable oil to reach one-third of the way up and set it over a medium-high heat. When it reaches 180°C, add a batch of 3–4 fritters and fry for 3–4 minutes until golden and crispy. Drain on kitchen paper, then season with salt and smoked paprika.

LEAVES

When I was putting this book together, I couldn't decide if leaves should have their own chapter separate from vegetables. As you can see, I finally decided that they should. In my head I think about them as separate entities (though leaves are, of course, vegetables). There's such a variety of leaves: think about the acidity of sorrel, the bitterness of treviso, the sweetness of soft-leaved lettuces. If you look at a delicate pea shoot or a bunch of robust ruby chard, it's obvious that there's a huge selection of flavours and textures. It's good to take a new perspective on them, as I hope I have here, as when you see familiar things in a slightly different light, you'll use them in a slightly different way. It's good to give them their own window of appreciation, to wake people up to their versatility, rather than just throwing them in a bowl with some vinegar.

Salads, like soup, sometimes get an undeservedly swift dismissal when people are choosing from a restaurant menu. They aren't seen as sexy, or culinarily adventurous, but instead are thought of as something you can quickly assemble at home rather than anything you might want to order when you go out to eat. Yet I am always drawn to salad at the start of a meal and I eat one at least once a day. The crisp textures, the pleasing acidity of the dressing and a well-made salad's plethora of counterpoints make for a

dish that both satisfies and renders every mouthful different and interesting. It is in many ways the ideal start to a meal, and achieving a perfectly balanced leaf salad is testimony to the skill of a cook.

The joy of salads is this juxtaposition of their elements: crunchy leaves tangled with soft ripe fruit, the savouriness of toasted nuts, the sweet-and-sour of a crisp vinaigrette, the lasting tang of cheese shavings, that burst of fragrance when you bite into fresh herbs. (For this reason, keep herb leaves whole or at least in large pieces whenever adding them to a salad; don't chop them into lawn-clippings anonymity.)

And there are so many salad leaves to choose from. Butterhead lettuce is gentle and yielding, perfect for a light summer dish when paired with other British vegetables. Rocket, watercress and land cress are peppery and arresting dark leaves: fantastic against other robust flavours. Gem and Romaine lettuces are ideal for their sheer crunch, either chopped fine or used as a vessel for other ingredients. (Try topping whole leaves with different fillings, almost like a taco... Feta, watermelon, mint and green olive perhaps? Or ricotta, broad beans, mint and lime zest?)

Winter is the season for bitter leaves, the majority of which come from Italy. The variety is vast: *tardivo*, *treviso*, *puntarella*, *grumulo*, *barbucine* and *castelfranco* to name just a handful. They are invariably beautiful to look at, flecked with scarlet and cream and twisted or frilled into fantastic shapes, but they do need an assured touch from the cook to turn them into something palatable. They are fantastic with other strong flavours such as anchovies or other oily fish, grilled red meat or salty cheese. They can be absolutely drenched with dressing; in fact they positively need it. To prepare them, discard the fibrous outer leaves and use the more tender, succulent inner layers, placing them into iced water to help crisp the leaves and to temper their bitterness.

Sometimes the more fibrous wintry leaves can take a bit longer in the oven. Kale can be good cooked long and slow, or added to stews, when it gains a lovely velvety, pasta-like mouthfeel. You can braise or bake certain lettuces, too. Leaves such as endives can be coloured in foaming butter, salted and sugared, then baked. This softens their bitterness and they become quite yielding, but still retain a little bit of juiciness in the stem. We tend to think of them as only a salad ingredient, but they can become the basis for a hearty meal.

Cabbages can equally be used in salads if shredded fine, though in this chapter we serve the sweet Hispi variety in all its sweet glory, as a generous wedge baked until tender then laced with buttery smoked eel that will fill all the crevasses.

Hopefully, with the direct approach I've taken to the recipes and the efficiency of the methods, the time you save in the kitchen can be spent sourcing the best ingredients. Find a greengrocer or online supplier: you only have to make the discovery once, then you can enjoy supporting them as a regular customer. Try new things: there's so much more to gain than there is to lose. The worst that can happen is that you have one mealtime you don't love; the best is that you make a discovery you can enjoy for the rest of your life. Imagine, for a moment, that you had never tasted basil, for instance… Try buying one variety of leaf on each shopping trip that you wouldn't usually buy. These little discoveries can raise a smile, make cooking a bit more fun and be enlightening, broadening your cooking knowledge.

Incredibly versatile, assuredly healthy and often inexpensive, leaves have deservedly moved ever closer to centre stage on our plates.

GRILLED RUNNER BEANS, NECTARINES, MINT & RICOTTA

When cooked over a barbecue or chargrill, runner beans become particularly savoury and flavoursome. Blanching them first ensures they are cooked through and tender within. Although it looks like a lot of salt in the water, remember they are only cooking in this very briefly, so the seasoning needs to penetrate in a very short amount of time. (In general, the briefer the blanching, the more salt is needed in the water.) The combination of smoked almonds, sweet nectarines, creamy ricotta and fresh herbs here makes for a memorable summer salad; a good salad is all about contrasts.

I always call coarse nut pastes 'pralines', though I do admit that this savoury version contains no sugar.

RUNNER BEANS

20 runner beans

olive oil

fine sea salt

sea salt flakes

BAKED NECTARINES

3 tablespoons olive oil

2 tablespoons caster sugar

2 tablespoons Chardonnay vinegar

juice of 1 lemon

4 ripe nectarines, quartered and pitted

SMOKED ALMOND PRALINE

200g smoked almonds

100g extra virgin olive oil

1 small garlic clove, crushed

ASSEMBLE

4 handfuls of mixed leaves (mesclun)

8 tablespoons Lemon dressing (see page 294)

finely grated zest of 1 lemon

200g ricotta (if it's slightly dry, mix in some cream to moisten, see page 274)

16 basil leaves

32 mint leaves

unsprayed edible flowers, such as geranium, cornflowers, dianthus or pea flowers (if available)

RUNNER BEANS

- Blanch the runner beans in rapidly boiling salted water (use 20g salt for each 1 litre of water) for 1 minute.
- Drain, refresh in iced water, drain again and place on sheets of kitchen paper. Top and tail the beans, then peel away the fibrous strings that run along both sides of each.
- Roll in olive oil and char on a hot chargrill pan (or a barbecue, if you have one) on both sides. Remove and keep in a single layer so they don't keep cooking in their own steam.
- Cut on the diagonal into lengths of 7–8cm (roughly 3 per bean), then season generously with sea salt flakes.

BAKED NECTARINES

- Preheat the oven to 120°C.
- Warm the olive oil, sugar, vinegar and lemon juice with 1 tablespoon water in a saucepan to dissolve the sugar and combine all the ingredients.
- Mix the nectarine quarters with this and place on a baking tray.
- Cook in the low oven for 30 minutes until tender, then remove and cool to room temperature.

SMOKED ALMOND PRALINE

- Increase the oven temperature to 170°C.
- Place the almonds in the oven and toast for 10–15 minutes until golden.
- Blend the nuts with the olive oil, garlic and a pinch of fine sea salt, on a low speed, to a coarse rubble.

ASSEMBLE

- Dress the beans and leaves generously with the lemon dressing and grated lemon zest.
- Spoon 2 tablespoons of the almond praline organically over the base of a plate, then scatter around the dressed runner beans, leaves, nectarines and blobs of ricotta.
- Scatter over and around the basil, mint and edible flowers, if using.

CANDY BEETROOT, RASPBERRIES, FETA & ALMONDS

A vibrant summer salad. Candy beetroot lack the earthiness of regular beetroot and are sweeter and somehow more summery in flavour, marrying beautifully with red fruits. Like any good salad, this is full of counterpoints: simultaneously soft and crisp, sweet and salty. In autumn, try it with regular beetroot, tarragon, hazelnuts and blackberries.

BEETROOT

4–6 candy beetroot, depending on size
fine sea salt

RASPBERRY DRESSING

150g raspberries
2 tablespoons Chardonnay vinegar
1 tablespoon caster sugar
6 tablespoons olive oil
juice of ½ lemon
1 teaspoon fennel seeds, lightly crushed
pinch of fine sea salt
pinch of black pepper

ALMONDS

100g almonds, unpeeled

ASSEMBLE

4 handfuls of mixed leaves
150g feta cheese, crumbled
handful of mint leaves (12 per person)

BEETROOT

~ Place the beetroot in a large pan of water, deep enough to cover them.
~ Simmer for about 90 minutes until tender, then drain. Leave until warm enough to handle, then peel.
~ Cut into large pieces, season with salt and dress while still warm in the raspberry dressing.

RASPBERRY DRESSING

~ Crush half the raspberries with a fork and mix in the remaining ingredients.
~ Add the remaining whole raspberries.

ALMONDS

~ Preheat the oven to 170°C. Spread the almonds out on a baking tray and toast in the oven for 10–15 minutes, or until lightly golden, then remove and cool. Roughly slice them; they should be small enough to mix with the other salad components, but need to retain identity and crunch.

ASSEMBLE

~ Mix the leaves gently with the beetroot and dressing, being careful not to crush the whole berries.
~ Scatter over a platter or individual dishes, then sprinkle over the feta, almonds, salad leaves and mint.

MUSHROOM SHAVINGS, OREGANO, PINE NUTS & PRESERVED LEMON

94

This salad is woody and earthy, primal and satisfying. Argan oil is a Moroccan delicacy with a nutty taste. Argan trees are notoriously prickly, so the farmers leave the fruit to fall to earth instead of manually picking it from the branch. The oil is made from the toasted kernel of the stone within. It's a lengthy and laborious process, hence the cost of the oil, but a little goes a long way and its growing popularity has also given a welcome boost to the Moroccan economy. So it's good for us and it's good for them, too.

There are many types of bitter leaf, and they are an acquired taste, but they are always mellowed by a vinegary dressing. They come into their own in salads such as these, where a sweeter, milder leaf would be overpowered by the other flavours.

If fresh oregano is unavailable, substitute it with fresh rosemary instead, or use 1 teaspoon dried oregano.

8 tablespoons pine nuts

80g argan oil

1 tablespoon chopped preserved lemon

2 tablespoons white wine vinegar

1 tablespoon clear honey

4 tablespoons oregano leaves

250g chestnut mushrooms, washed (see page 80) and finely sliced on a mandolin

4 handfuls of bitter leaves, such as frisee

fine sea salt

―――

~ Toast the pine nuts in the argan oil in a frying pan over a medium heat until light golden, then transfer to a bowl and season lightly. Leave to cool.

~ Mix in the preserved lemon, vinegar, honey and oregano.

~ Gently mix the mushrooms and bitter leaves together, then dress with the pine nut dressing.

~ Scatter over a large platter, or serve on individual plates.

SALAD OF ROCKET COURGETTE, MINT, PISTACHIO & FETA

This dressing is perfect with barbecued lamb chops or oily fish. When courgettes are marinated in a light vinaigrette from raw, they retain their buttery bite and transform into something elegant, while their collected juices become a dressing that brings the dish together.

DRESSING

20g mint leaves

10g basil leaves

20g baby spinach

2 tablespoons toasted pistachios
(see page 19)

½ garlic clove, crushed

75g extra virgin olive oil

30g feta cheese, crumbled

pinch of caster sugar

pinch of fine sea salt

COURGETTE

courgettes: green, yellow and *trombetta*, if available, allowing ½ per person

courgette flowers, if available

8 tablespoons Lemon dressing
(see page 294)

ASSEMBLE

4 handfuls of rocket

1 tablespoon Lemon dressing
(see page 294)

4 tablespoons toasted pistachios

DRESSING

- Blend everything together for 10 seconds into a coarse pesto.

COURGETTE

- Thinly slice the courgettes into both rounds and lengths, both about 3mm thick, on a mandolin. Tear the courgette flowers, if using.

~ Season generously with salt and lemon dressing and leave for 10 minutes to wilt. Save the juices that will come from the courgettes.

ASSEMBLE

~ Lightly dress the rocket leaves in the lemon dressing.

~ Scatter the courgette shavings around the plate, then spoon over blobs of the dressing and the juices that came from the courgettes.

~ Scatter over the toasted pistachios, rocket and torn courgette flowers, if using.

SALAD OF BUTTERHEAD LETTUCE, AVOCADO, GOOSEBERRIES, MARJORAM & CARAMELISED PECANS

A quirky and delicious salad, combining tart gooseberries with smooth avocados, sweet pecans, fragrant marjoram and milky lettuce. I usually recommend a light touch with marjoram, though the other components of this salad can stand up to it. Butterhead lettuce is gentle and refreshing, with very little bitterness.

The name 'lettuce' is derived from its Latin name Lactuca sativa, *in turn derived from the Latin* lac *for 'milk', due to the milky colour of the liquid you see when you cut into the stem.*

GOOSEBERRY COMPOTE

300g gooseberries

45g elderflower cordial

30g caster sugar

juice of ½ lemon

PECANS

100g pecans

50g caster sugar

pinch of fine sea salt

ASSEMBLE

2 Butterhead lettuces

2 ripe avocados, pitted and peeled

8 tablespoons Lemon dressing (see page 294)

16 sweet dessert gooseberries, halved

2 tablespoons marjoram leaves

elderflower head (optional)

GOOSEBERRY COMPOTE

~ Place all the ingredients in a saucepan with 45g water, cover and cook for 10 minutes at a simmer, then remove the lid and cook until you have a light compote. Cool to room temperature.

PECANS

~ Preheat the oven to 170°C. Toast the nuts on a baking tray for 10 minutes. Lay out a sheet of baking parchment.

~ Caramelise the sugar in a saucepan until an amber or copper colour. Add the salt and pecans and stir to coat.

~ Add 3 tablespoons hot water. This will dissolve the caramel. Boil away the water until the caramel is glossy but you can still separate the pecans.

~ Transfer to the prepared sheet of baking parchment to cool.

ASSEMBLE

~ Remove tired outer leaves from the lettuces and separate the inner leaves. Wash in iced water and spin dry.

~ Cut the avocados into thick slices.

~ Place the lettuce and avocados in a mixing bowl and dress generously with the lemon dressing.

~ Gently mix in the compote, halved gooseberries, marjoram and pecans, then place on a platter, or in a salad bowl, with elderflowerlets, if using.

CREAMED SPINACH ON GRANARY TOAST, SOFT-BOILED EGG

Creamed spinach is a something of a forgotten favourite: always enjoyed on the rare occasions it is served, but seldom written about. It's not new. It's not trendy. It is, however, delicious.

I don't often cook with black pepper, but here its warmth, with the nutmeg, make the dish. It is fine to use baby spinach, but the larger-leafed variety will give a bit more body.

Do read the recipe for the soft-boiled eggs for perfect results: a large pan of water and room-temperature eggs are key.

SPINACH

80g salted butter

750g spinach, ideally large-leafed rather than baby, washed

½ large white onion, ideally, or brown, finely chopped

2 cloves

1 large garlic clove, crushed

1½ tablespoons plain flour

300g whole milk

225g whipping cream

nutmeg, finely grated

12 turns of black pepper

fine sea salt

EGGS

4 eggs, at room temperature

sea salt flakes

black pepper

ASSEMBLE

8 slices of malted granary bread

salted butter

SPINACH

- Put a metal baking tray in the freezer.
- Melt half the butter in a pan, then add the spinach, season lightly with salt, then cover and cook until the leaves have wilted, stirring every so often so it cooks evenly.
- Drain in a colander, then spread on the frozen tray to cool quickly. Chill the tray in the refrigerator until cold.
- Squeeze out as much water as you can from the spinach, using both hands, then transfer to a clean tea towel and wring out any remaining liquid. Roughly chop the leaves.
- Melt the remaining butter in a saucepan over a medium heat and sweat the onion and cloves for 10 minutes, covered, until softened but not coloured.
- Remove the cloves, then add the garlic and stir. Cook for 30 seconds, then add the flour and bring to a simmer.
- Gradually whisk in the milk until smooth, then gently simmer for 2–3 minutes. Add the cream, then whisk again until smooth and boiling. Now tip in the spinach and mix.
- Season well with nutmeg and black pepper; it may also need a pinch more salt. Cook for another couple of minutes until thick and glossy. Keep warm while you cook the eggs.

EGGS

- Bring a large saucepan of water to the boil over a high heat. The pan must be sufficiently big that the water remains boiling once the eggs are added.
- Add the eggs, then set a timer to 5 minutes if the eggs are medium or 6 minutes if large, and prepare a large bowl of iced water.
- Once the eggs are cooked, remove from the water with a slotted spoon and plunge into the cold water. You want to cool them on the outside just enough so you can hold and peel them, but they should still be warm within. Peel carefully, slice in half, then season with salt and black pepper.

ASSEMBLE

- Toast the bread, then butter it. Place on a plate and divide the creamed spinach on top.
- Top with the boiled egg halves and serve immediately.

SPRING ONIONS, GOAT'S CURD, PISTACHIO & GRAPEFRUIT

This looks like a lot of raw onions, but once they are crisped in iced water and tossed in lemon dressing, they are mellow and flavoursome rather than acrid and aggressive. They can take a lot of dressing and zest, so don't be shy. If you remain unconvinced, you can replace them with fennel and / or radish shavings.

Like raw onions, coriander can be polarising, so feel free to substitute it as you wish with mint, basil or lemon verbena; or marigold leaf, if you have some growing and unsprayed, would be absolutely delicious! If goat's curd is unavailable, find a soft goat's milk cheese and mix it with yogurt to soften the taste and texture.

SPRING ONIONS

2 bunches of large spring onions

PISTACHIO PRALINE

200g unsalted shelled pistachios

120g extra virgin olive oil

1 garlic clove, crushed

pinch of fine sea salt

ASSEMBLE

1 pink grapefruit

8 tablespoons Lemon dressing (see page 294)

150g goat's curd

1 bunch of coriander, leaves picked, stems finely sliced

SPRING ONIONS

~ Trim the spring onions and finely slice on an angle, then put them in a colander sitting within a bowl.

~ Wash under cold running water for 10 minutes, then transfer to a big bowl of iced water to crisp until required.

PISTACHIO PRALINE

~ Preheat the oven to 170°C.

~ Toss half the pistachios on a baking sheet with 2 tablespoons of the olive oil and roast for 10 minutes until golden.

~ Blend with the remaining olive oil, garlic and salt to a coarse purée.

~ Roughly chop the remaining pistachios and mix them in.

ASSEMBLE

~ Drain the onions and put them in a bowl. Salt lightly, then grate over the grapefruit zest. Segment the grapefruit (see page 69) and halve each piece.

~ Dress the spring onions heavily with the lemon dressing.

~ Spread 2 tablespoons of the pistachio praline across the base of each plate.

~ Scatter over blobs of the goat's curd, then add 6 grapefruit pieces to each.

~ Sprinkle over the coriander stems and spring onion salad, then top with the coriander leaves.

BAKED HISPI CABBAGE WITH SMOKED EEL, GARLIC & PARSLEY BUTTER

108

A quick and easy dish for a cold Sunday night. Hispi cabbage is incredibly versatile, equally delicious shredded raw into a salad, lightly steamed, or baked in a hot oven as it is here. It is often called 'sweetheart cabbage' in the supermarkets, for the mild, sweet flavour of its central leaves. It's definitely worth trying even if you think you don't like cabbage. If smoked eel is unavailable, this is delicious with brown shrimps, or smoked salmon.

CABBAGE

1 Hispi cabbage

4 tablespoons virgin rapeseed or sunflower oil

fine sea salt

GARLIC & EEL BUTTER

50g salted butter

1 garlic clove, crushed

2 tablespoons roughly chopped parsley leaves

finely grated zest and juice of ½ lemon

150g hot-smoked eel fillet, chopped into 1cm pieces

CABBAGE

~ Preheat the oven to 190°C.

~ Trim the outer leaves from the cabbage, then cut it into quarters through the core.

~ Brush with the oil and season lightly with salt, then place on a lightly oiled roasting tray.

~ Cover with foil and bake the cabbage in the hot oven for 15 minutes, then remove the foil and bake for a further 10–15 minutes, until tender within and light golden on the outside.

GARLIC & EEL BUTTER

~ Gently melt the butter, then add the remaining ingredients just to warm them through; after all, the hot-smoked eel is already cooked.

TO SERVE

~ Remove the cabbage from the oven and transfer to warmed plates, then spoon over the butter. Evenly distribute the pieces of smoked eel and make sure they fall between the layers of the baked cabbage.

SHELLFISH

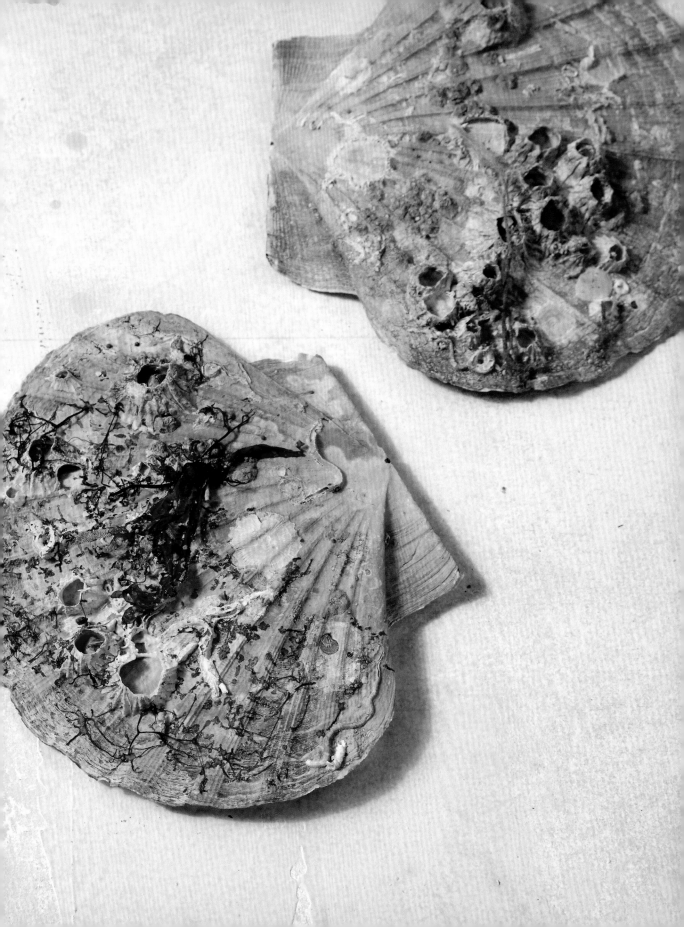

112

Shellfish has a depth of flavour and textural viscerality incomparable to any other food, which explains why some people have a love:hate relationship with it, or at least with any one type. The variety is enormous, from the ozone-fresh salinity and slippery texture of a native oyster, to the firm sweetness and near-meatiness of a jumbo Scottish langoustine. The shellfish of the British Isles are often specific to certain parts: incredible scallops come from Orkney, brown shrimps from Morecambe Bay, squid, crab and lobster from Cornwall. Oysters are now successfully farmed in various locations, but my two favourites are rock oysters from Porthilly, at the estuary of the River Camel, and native oysters from Colchester. The rocks are available all year round, the natives in any month with an 'r' in it (which basically means not during the summer).

However, shellfish can be quite intimidating to prepare at home; their shells can feel like a physical barrier. So I thought it would be helpful to give a few basic tips here for handling the most common types, which I hope should make it easier.

For mussels, simply pull away the straggly 'beards' from the shells and cook them in boiling wine or water, or even just in a hot dry pan with a lid on top (though cooking them in a small amount of water and wine gives a lovely stock).

Remember to always strain their cooking liquor through a fine sieve, or a double layer of muslin or new J-cloth, to remove any grit, and to always discard the last couple of tablespoons of liquor from the pan, as that is where the majority of any detritus will collect. Treat cockles and clams in much the same way, though no de-bearding is needed for those. Aside from steaming, all these bivalves are also delicious cooked in a very hot oven, under a preheated grill or over charcoal, as in the recipe in this chapter. With all of them, discard any shells that are cracked before cooking, or that are open and refuse to close when tapped on the edge of a sink, or any that remain closed after cooking.

Whenever opening oysters, always use an oyster knife and make sure the hand with which you are holding the oyster is well protected with a folded tea towel, so you can't accidentally stab yourself. Also make sure the oyster is nicely stabilised on another folded tea towel. Once the shell has been prised open, cut the flesh away from the flat shell where it is attached. I always feel that serving oysters is very dependent on context. By the seaside, they taste infinitely better! They also have to be ice cold.

When cooking prawns, always remember to save the heads, as they are full of flavour and make an amazing sauce or stock, especially when roasted.

In this chapter, they are served both inside a gram flour pancake and also potted; both of these techniques extend an expensive ingredient as well as really maximising its flavour.

Crab is an item that is not prohibitively costly, but – in my opinion – the real luxury lies in getting all the prep work done for you by a fishmonger. Having all the meat already cooked, flaked and checked for stray pieces of shell makes the whole experience far more enjoyable than doing it yourself. OK, I know that some people find the process of breaking a crab down fun (and you can find many tutorials that show the lengthy and slightly tricky process online), but having prepared so many crabs as a chef, it feels an awful lot like work to me! I personally far prefer white crab meat to brown for its purer, sweeter flavour. In this chapter, crab is gently warmed in garlic butter and served in a baked baby pumpkin, much as you would eat a filled jacket potato.

Squid is technically categorised as a cephalopod, like octopus and cuttlefish. The latter are perhaps less likely to be cooked at home as they require long braising, whereas squid provides a meal in minutes and is fantastic both fresh and frozen; I find the recipe with Thai basil, ginger and garlic in the next few pages is incredibly addictive.

I only recommend using scallops if they are large, diver-caught and in the shell.

Dredged scallops are both full of grit and terrible for the health of the seabed, while pre-shucked scallops are invariably waterlogged and therefore impossible to caramelise. To shuck scallops, using a knife with a thin blade, insert it between the two shells where they are hinged together and slice open, angling the blade towards the flat shell where the meat is attached so you can extract it all. Scallops are usually best pan-fried the day after opening. When at their freshest, they can actually feel quite tight, even when undercooked. A day in the refrigerator between some sheets of kitchen paper will relax the flesh and give a nicer caramelisation. Always use the heaviest pan you have when frying scallops, to give a deep and even golden colour; a lightweight pan just doesn't produce the same result.

The overarching rule for all shellfish is not to overcook them, or they will lose all their elegance and textural pleasure. Also, other than scallops or prawns, there is little need for seasoning, or just a light touch if at all; their natural salinity will be sufficient.

GRILLED SHELLFISH WITH SAMPHIRE, NEW POTATOES, THYME & GIROLLES

Shellfish, when raw, are briny, slippery and wet. Cooked this way, under a blisteringly hot grill, they are transformed from something delicate into a dish that is far meatier and bolder, while maintaining their delicious salinity. This is incredibly simple to make, but you do need a raging hot grill to get the best results, or it can also be made very successfully over a hot barbecue.

100g olive oil

75g white wine

2 garlic cloves, crushed

2 tablespoons roughly chopped thyme leaves

1kg mixed shellfish, such as mussels, clams, cockles and razor clams, washed

500g cooked new potatoes, some sliced vertically, others sliced across

200g girolles, or other wild mushrooms, or shiitake, halved or quartered if large, lightly washed (see page 80)

100g samphire

1cm fresh horseradish root, finely grated

½ lemon

~ Preheat the grill to its maximum setting and set a roasting tray inside to heat up.

~ Mix together the olive oil, wine, garlic and thyme in a large bowl, then add the shellfish, potatoes and mushrooms and mix well. Place in a single layer on the hot roasting tray and return to the grill.

~ Cook until the shellfish have opened, the potatoes are warmed and the mushrooms softened, about 5 minutes, depending on the strength of the grill.

~ Meanwhile, bring a large saucepan of unsalted water to the boil and add the samphire. Blanch for 10 seconds, then drain in a colander.

~ Grate the horseradish evenly over the shellfish, potatoes and mushrooms, then grate on the lemon zest, finally squeezing over the lemon juice.

~ Mix in the still-warm samphire, then divide between warmed serving plates, or serve on a warmed platter.

GRAM FLOUR PANCAKE WITH GARLIC SHRIMPS, FENNEL & PARSLEY

116

You could use this pancake mix with anything: anchovies, baked root vegetables, chorizo… It is simple to make and absolutely delicious, with the savoury kick of street food, and is just as satisfying. The pancake stretches the protein further, creating a substantial meal out of a small amount of fish.

Do use smoked rapeseed oil if possible; it is now readily available online and, as our tastes evolve, so too do the ingredients at our disposal. The smokiness of the pancake is a great contrast to the crisp, sharp fennel slaw.

A poached or soft-boiled egg would also work well with this. If brown shrimps are available, do use them; they are intensely savoury and worth the extra pennies.

Serves 4 as a starter, or 2 as a light lunch

FENNEL

300g fennel (1 very large or 2 smaller bulbs), halved, then finely sliced

100g spring onions (about ½ bunch), finely sliced on an angle

½ teaspoon fine sea salt

½ teaspoon caster sugar

juice of ½ lemon

2 tablespoons Chardonnay vinegar

100g Mayonnaise (see page 294)

100g Greek yogurt

1 tablespoon finely sliced parsley leaves

50g Lilliput or nonpareille capers, rinsed

PANCAKE

110g gram flour

pinch of cayenne pepper

pinch of baking powder

150g peeled shrimps, ideally brown shrimps

1 garlic clove, finely grated

smoked rapeseed oil

sea salt flakes

FENNEL

- Mix the fennel, spring onions, salt, sugar, lemon juice and Chardonnay vinegar together and leave for 1 hour.
- Drain off half the juice.
- Mix in the remaining ingredients, then check the seasoning.

PANCAKE

- Preheat the grill to its maximum setting before you start cooking.
- Whisk together the gram flour, cayenne and baking powder with a pinch of fine sea salt, then gradually pour in 250g water, whisking as you do so, to create a batter. Add the shrimps and garlic.
- Heat a nonstick frying pan, then add 2 tablespoons smoked rapeseed oil.
- Pour in half the pancake mix, making sure you get a fair amount of the shrimps in each pancake. Colour lightly on the bottom, then finish cooking the top side under the hot grill (if your grill is not powerful, you can also finish this in a hot oven, preheated to its highest temperature).

- You can serve it like this (golden side uppermost), but you do get a much better taste if you fry the side with all the shrimps on too, after grilling. To do so, flip the pancake out on to a baking tray and then return the pan to a high heat. Add another 2 tablespoons oil to the pan, then slide the pancake off the baking tray and into the hot oil, colouring for a minute or so until the shrimps toast in the smoky oil.
- Season generously with more smoked oil and some sea salt flakes. Remove from the pan and cut into wedges.
- Repeat with the remaining half of the pancake batter.

TO SERVE

- Serve the pancakes straightaway with a generous spoon of the dressed fennel alongside.

CRISPY SQUID WITH THAI BASIL, GINGER & GARLIC

Crispy squid is a go-to on late-night takeaway menus, yet very simple to make, too. This sauce is as addictive as it is utterly inauthentic, with rounded, savoury oyster sauce and butter, fragrant ginger and herbs and black pepper heat. Scoring the squid is vital, giving more surface area for crisping and for the sauce.

SQUID

500g medium squid, bodies cut into pieces about 7cm (credit card-sized)

SAUCE

20g root ginger, peeled and chopped

20g garlic, roughly chopped

30g coriander leaf, stem and root, washed and chopped, plus more to serve

30g Thai basil leaves, plus more to serve

60g oyster sauce

20g caster sugar

1 tablespoon crushed black pepper

200g unsalted butter, melted

sea salt flakes

SPRING ONIONS

½ bunch of spring onions

ASSEMBLE

1 litre vegetable oil

200g cornflour

lime wedges, to serve

SQUID

~ Score the squid pieces with a sharp knife, to create a cross-hatch.

SAUCE

~ Blend all the ingredients together with a pinch of salt for 10 seconds in a blender.

SPRING ONIONS

~ Slice the spring onions as finely as you can, to create long, thin pieces. Keep in iced water until needed.

ASSEMBLE

~ Heat a large saucepan with the vegetable oil to 180°C. Have the sauce warm and melted in another pan.

~ Mix the cornflour and 2 teaspoons salt, coat the squid and dust off excess.

~ Deep-fry in the hot oil in batches for 1 minute, or until light golden, moving the pieces so they cook evenly.

~ Drain on kitchen paper and season with salt flakes. Toss in the sauce and drained spring onions and serve with sea salt flakes and lime wedges.

BAKED PUMPKIN WITH WARM CRAB & MELTED BUTTER

Crab works brilliantly with vegetables that have a natural sweetness. Here, baby pumpkins are gently baked in the oven until tender, then filled with buttery warm crab. Given the nature of the tiny flakes of crab meat, it can absorb plenty of dairy, almost like a risotto. It is key to pick over crab to check for shell prior to cooking. To do this, spread it very thinly on a tray over ice and press down with your fingers. Have a bowl of water alongside to place any shell into. I love the juiciness and clean sweet flavour of white crab meat. If you can't find small pumpkins, you can bake the mixture in the bulbous bases of butternut squashes instead.

PUMPKIN

4 small pumpkins, such as Jack-be-Little, ideally no less than 300g each (or see recipe introduction)

4 tablespoons virgin rapeseed oil

fine sea salt

CRAB

100g salted butter

1 garlic clove, crushed

200g white crab meat, picked and checked (see recipe introduction)

1 tablespoon roughly chopped parsley leaves

finely grated zest of up to 1 lemon

basil leaves, to serve (optional)

PUMPKIN

- Preheat the oven to 160°C.
- Wipe the pumpkins with a damp cloth to remove any earth. Cut the tops off the pumpkins, taking off just enough to form a sturdy lid. (You need a deep base so there will be enough space for the crab filling.) Scoop out the seeds neatly with a tablespoon.
- Place the bases and matching lids side by side on a baking tray lined with baking parchment.
- Brush the pumpkins generously all over with virgin rapeseed oil, then season all over with salt.
- Bake for 30–60 minutes, depending on the variety of pumpkin you are using, until completely tender but still holding their shape.

CRAB

- Heat the butter in a pan and add the garlic; fry for 30 seconds, being careful that it gets no colour, then add the crab and mix. Add the parsley, with salt and lemon zest to taste.

TO SERVE

- Spoon the crab into the pumpkins, arrange over some basil leaves, if using, then top with the lids.

MALTED PIKELETS WITH WARM POTTED SHRIMPS

Brown shrimps can stand up to anything; they're delicious with Indian spices, or tossed with buttery pasta.

PIKELETS

360g whole milk

1 teaspoon malt extract

1 teaspoon caster sugar

8g fresh yeast, or 4g dried yeast

150g strong white bread flour

100g plain wholemeal flour

6g fine sea salt

1 tablespoon virgin rapeseed oil

sunflower oil, to fry

julienned spring onions (optional)

SHRIMPS

200g salted butter

150g peeled brown shrimps

pinch of ground mace

pinch of cayenne pepper

¼ garlic clove, crushed

juice of ¼ lemon

¼ cucumber, peeled, deseeded and finely chopped

1 teaspoon Chardonnay vinegar

2 tablespoons chopped parsley leaves

2 tablespoons samphire, picked and blanched for 10 seconds in boiling water

pinch of fine sea salt

PIKELETS

~ Warm the milk to 40°C (just above body temperature), then remove from the heat and whisk in the malt extract, sugar and yeast to dissolve.

~ Mix both flours and the salt in a bowl, then whisk in the warm milk, followed by the rapeseed oil. Cover and leave to prove at room temperature until doubled in size, about 45 minutes.

~ Place a nonstick frying pan over a medium heat with a small amount of sunflower oil.

~ Take a small ladle of the mixture for each pikelet and fry, in batches, for 2–3 minutes on each side, until light golden and cooked within. Transfer to a warmed plate while you cook the rest.

SHRIMPS

~ Warm the butter until melted but not foaming and pour it over the shrimps, spices, garlic and lemon juice in a bowl. Stir to allow the flavours to combine.

~ Mix the cucumber, salt and vinegar in a bowl and leave for 15 minutes.

~ Stir the cucumber, parsley and samphire into the potted shrimps.

TO SERVE

~ Place a warm pikelet on each plate and spoon over the shrimps, adding julienned spring onions, if you like.

GRILLED SCALLOPS, CRUSHED PEAS & MINT

126

This is my version of a great combination, made famous a long time ago by Rowley Leigh at Kensington Place. I went there for my sixteenth birthday for a truly memorable meal; it was simultaneously delicious, accessible and devoid of fuss and ceremony. Proper cooking, as chefs would say. My mum made the booking and must have told them I wanted to be a chef, as on arrival, there was a lovely note from Rowley to get in touch. The next summer, having just sat my GCSEs and probably not even shaving yet, I joined the brigade as a holiday job and loved every minute.

Here, the sweetness of the scallops marries perfectly with that of the peas, the mint punching through to elevate the dish into a beautifully balanced modern classic. Hats off, Rowley! I only ever buy scallops in the shell; they cost more but are worth it. Buy larger scallops, because that thickness of flesh will highlight their meatiness. They keep well in the freezer, so if you come across them, feel free to buy more than you need and freeze them. Opening a scallop for the first time might feel like a leap into the unknown, so I've given a step-by-step guide.

PEAS

400g frozen petits pois, defrosted

80g extra virgin olive oil

1 teaspoon caster sugar

pinch of fine sea salt

MINT SAUCE

50g Chardonnay vinegar

15g caster sugar

15g mint leaves, finely chopped

pinch of fine sea salt

SCALLOPS

4 extra-large scallops in the shells

2 tablespoons extra virgin olive oil

1 garlic clove, halved

¼ lemon

ASSEMBLE

coarse salt, small sea shells or seaweed, to stabilise the scallop shells

12 mint tips

12 pea shoots

———

PEAS

~ Pulse all the ingredients in a food processor until crushed, about 10 seconds. Transfer to a small saucepan.

MINT SAUCE

~ Bring 50g water, the vinegar, sugar and salt to the boil in a saucepan, stirring to ensure the sugar and salt dissolve, then remove from the heat and add the mint. Leave to cool.

SCALLOPS

- Take a filleting knife in your preferred hand and a scallop in your other. Have the split in the scallop shell (which should be tightly closed) pointing down and the hinge pointing up: it is safer for the knife to hit the board than to go flying through the air. The flat shell should be touching your thumb and the curved side touching your other 4 fingers.

- Place the point of the knife into the split in the shell at the very top and cut down in a swift movement, angling the blade against the flat shell to make sure you take off all the meat.

- The scallop should now be sitting on its curved shell. There will be a black sack. Hook your index finger inside that and pull it out. It will bring with it the remainder of the scallop insides.

- The white circle of scallop has a small white muscle alongside it. Place a spoon between scallop and shell and scoop under to remove it cleanly, then scrape off the muscle. Scrub the shell.

- You now have your perfectly prepped scallop and clean shell. Rinse the scallop quickly under cold water, then store it in a new J-cloth in the refrigerator. This will help to remove some of the moisture, which will in turn help it to caramelise in the pan. Repeat to shuck all the scallops.

- Warm the 4 curved scallop shells in a low oven (discard the flat shells).

- Heat the oil in a frying pan with the garlic, allow to sizzle for 30 seconds, then remove before it starts to colour.

- Salt the scallops well on both sides.

- Increase the temperature of the pan until very hot and add the scallops with their flatter, wider sides (the tops) facing down. Cook for 1 minute or so until nicely coloured with a golden crust, then turn over.

- Remove from the heat and finish cooking on the other side. The scallops should be just cooked, with colour on only one side. Remove from the pan to a warmed plate to rest.

- Add the lemon juice to the pan to emulsify with the oil, then pour it over the scallops to glaze.

- Carve each scallop into 4–5 slices vertically, or leave whole.

ASSEMBLE

- Place some coarse salt, small sea shells or seaweed in a bowl and use it to stabilise the warm scallop shells.

- Heat the crushed peas and place 2 large tablespoons in each shell.

- Top each with a scallop, then spoon over 1 tablespoon of the mint sauce.

- Scatter over the mint tips and pea shoots and serve immediately.

LOBSTER THERMIDOR
MACARONI CHEESE

Posh comfort food, essentially, best served with lots of chilled Champagne. This is a great mac and cheese recipe that is also delicious in its virginal form (without the lobster). As you make the dish, it looks quite wet, but as it cooks under the hot grill, the sauce soaks into the pasta. It is really important to keep the lobster in large chunks so it feels indulgent and doesn't get lost among the macaroni. Colouring it in a hot pan beforehand adds to the flavour (in the same way as colouring meat). As with all luxury ingredients, when you do use them, be generous, so they live up to their star billing.

As an alternative to pasta, the lobster and cheese sauce would be delicious with a jacket potato.

4 dressed lobsters, shelled

50g olive oil

50g Cognac or whisky

1 garlic clove, crushed

300g macaroni

40g salted butter

40g plain flour

500g whole milk

150g Cheddar, grated, plus 50g more for the top

60g Parmesan, grated, plus 30g more for the top

½ teaspoon ground mace

1 tablespoon Dijon mustard

pinch of fine sea salt

~ Cut the lobsters into large pieces. Heat the oil in a frying pan over a high heat, salt the lobsters lightly, then fry for 30 seconds, to toast the outsides. Deglaze the pan with the Cognac or whisky, then transfer the lobsters to a plate. Do this in batches if needed, so the pan stays hot and the lobsters colour rather than stew.

~ Fry the garlic lightly in a little of the oil, then pour it over the lobster.

~ Boil the macaroni for 8–10 minutes in a saucepan of boiling salted water (using 10g salt for each litre of water) or until al dente. Drain.

~ Heat the grill to its hottest setting.

~ Melt the butter in a saucepan and add the flour, whisking to combine. Gradually add the milk, whisking after each addition, until the sauce is smooth, making sure it comes to the boil so the flour is cooked out. Add the cheeses, mace and mustard and stir until melted, then mix in the macaroni and lobster, reserving a few lobster pieces to scatter on top.

~ Transfer to a gratin dish and top with the reserved lobster and extra cheese. Place under the hot grill to glaze the top, then serve immediately.

FISH

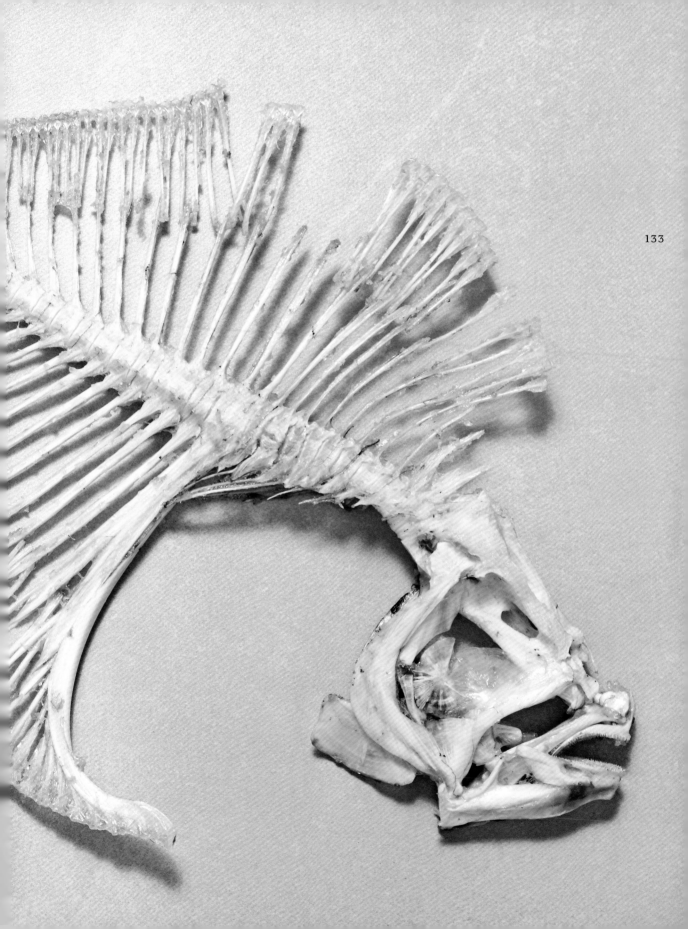

133

134

I've noticed that there is a distinct difference between the fish dishes that people enjoy when eating out and those they are comfortable to cook at home. Often, we cooks play it safe in our own kitchens, rather than exploring the many wonderful, slightly edgier possibilities.

You might gladly order and enjoy a delicious tuna tartare or cured salmon in a restaurant, but could lack the confidence to serve them in your own home, despite the fact that they are relatively simple to make. (Both recipes are in the pages that follow.) It's easier, many of us find, to revert to an underwhelming and unexciting old stalwart dish such as fish pie.

Granted, it can be hard to source the same quality of fish on the high street as restaurants are lucky enough to access, and I would always advise visiting a fishmonger over grabbing pre-packaged fish from a supermarket shelf.

When you are buying fish, target what looks best on the slab and work around it. You may have gone out looking for sea bream for a recipe, but if the sea bass looks better, buy that instead. The only real consideration is that you should substitute an oily fish for another oily fish, a flat fish for another flat fish, or a meaty white fish for another meaty white fish, as you wouldn't necessarily want to apply the same cooking techniques for one to the other.

When cooking and seasoning fish, you need a light touch to get the best out of it. Historically, there has been a bad habit of overcooking fish in this country. Often the temperature at which fish is perfectly cooked is considerably lower than for meats, by as much as 10°C. At my restaurant, we cook salmon until the core reaches 44°C and steam turbot to 46°C; to put that into perspective, this is less than 10°C above our own body temperature. It is quite surprising if you aren't aware, and very useful to know. (I recommend a Thermapen to measure the core temperatures of pieces of fish or meat, which is widely available.)

I generally prefer to cook oily fish over charcoal, in a scorching hot pan or under the grill, whereas I like white fish lightly steamed or simply baked. Skate is delicious roasted on the bone in a hot pan, which really accentuates its gelatinous and meaty texture; the grooves in the flesh make it perfect for receiving a poured-over tasty sauce or dressing that will permeate the fish. Monkfish is similarly meaty and is also brilliant cooked on the bone, though equally delicious gently poached, as for the bourride recipe in this chapter.

Bourride is a classic fish stew from the south of France, traditionally made with cheap oily fish; my version is more indulgent and refined, but very quick to assemble.

Salmon is fantastic served raw, and the one-hour cure you'll find in these pages is a perfect recipe for converting people who think they don't like raw fish. The seasoning and marinade suffuse the fish and firm the texture within this short time, transforming it into a meaty and richly palatable delicacy. Tuna is a fish probably now more renowned for its raw preparations than when it is cooked, and rightly so. Here it is mixed with figs and basil to create a delicious summer tartare. Feel free to use the fatty *toro* or tuna belly if you can get hold of it, though the red meat (*akame*) has an incredibly clean flavour and is the most readily available. Very high-quality tuna is deep-frozen at sea, so don't be put off if you find that the tuna on the fishmonger's slab is frozen, as the freezing process kills bacteria and preserves the flavour and colour of the fish. (The tartare recipe would also be delicious with sashimi-quality salmon.)

Turbot, plaice and sole are all flat fish, invariably best gently cooked to showcase their taste and texture. Plaice looks meaty, but cooks to a very soft flesh. Turbot is on the other end of the spectrum and actually benefits from a few days in the refrigerator before cooking, to allow the flesh to tenderise. I cook it simply with a delicious sauce made from its bones, which is then used to poach the fish. Turbot is expensive, so it makes complete sense to use every bit of it.

I've also included in this chapter a couple of recipes for cod: use the meaty neck end of the fillet for the crispy cod recipe and the thinner tail end pieces for the brandade. Brandade was originally made with the heavily salted cod you find in Portugal and Spain, though this version is much simpler and fresher, and is a favourite of many chefs, but rarely cooked at home. You should definitely make it, as it's delicious with roast peppers, pickles, or toasted flatbreads.

TUNA TARTARE WITH FIGS & BASIL

A sunny summer starter that makes a great first impression. Fish tartares are best served cold, so here the crushed ice is both practical and beautiful. Use the very best fish. Tuna would be my preference, but bream or salmon would also work. Remove any sinew or blood before chopping and don't cut it too small, as the mouthfeel of large dice is far more indulgent than something closer to mince.

The key to a tartare is to season, but not to overload, as the protein is the star and should be embellished, not overshadowed.

Feel free to substitute figs for apricots, plums, melon or pears.

BASIL EMULSION

50g basil (save smaller tips to serve)

200g Mayonnaise (see page 294)

200g Greek yogurt

2 tablespoons Chardonnay vinegar

TUNA

400g fresh tuna, chopped into
1cm cubes

finely grated zest and juice of
½ lemon

1 teaspoon fine sea salt

3 tablespoons extra virgin olive oil

ASSEMBLE

4 figs, finely sliced

crushed ice

BASIL EMULSION

~ Blend everything together, then keep in the refrigerator until needed

TUNA

~ Mix all the ingredients together just before serving and keep in a bowl set over crushed ice. Check the seasoning.

ASSEMBLE

~ Place 2 tablespoons of basil emulsion in the base of each serving bowl.

~ Divide the tuna tartare evenly on top, then pat it down to level the mixture.

~ Top with the fig slices to cover, then scatter over a few of the reserved basil tips.

~ Nestle these bowls within a larger bowl filled with crushed ice to serve.

WATERCRESS SOUP, SMOKED MACKEREL & POTATO SALAD

A soup may not excite on paper. A good soup, however, is a thing of beauty: a bowlful of comforting warmth with depth and purity. It was during my time at Le Manoir aux Quat' Saisons that I realised how good a soup could be, and a great deal of that is due to fast cooking: keeping ingredients fresh and capturing their flavours.

SOUP

½ white onion, finely chopped

1 leek, finely chopped

200g unpeeled new potatoes, chopped

60g salted butter

150g watercress, picked and washed

50g baby spinach, washed

400g ice cubes

fine sea salt

SALAD

500g Charlotte potatoes

150g Mayonnaise (see page 294)

1 tablespoon Chardonnay vinegar

1 tablespoon chopped parsley leaves

1 tablespoon chopped chives

1 tablespoon chopped gherkins

1 teaspoon wholegrain mustard

ASSEMBLE

8 smoked streaky bacon rashers

2 fillets of smoked mackerel, flaked

SOUP

~ Place 2 roasting trays in the freezer. Gently sweat the onion, leek and potatoes in half the butter for 15 minutes, covered, until softened.

~ Add 500g boiling water and 1 teaspoon salt, bring to the boil and simmer for 5 minutes until tender. Pour into a frozen tray. Leave to cool.

~ In another pan, wilt the watercress in the remaining butter for 2 minutes, then add the spinach and wilt for another 30 seconds; season lightly. Pour into the second frozen tray; add the ice cubes to arrest the cooking.

~ Blend the potato soup until smooth, then pass through a sieve. Repeat with the watercress soup, including all the ice and juices from the tray. Combine both soups and check the seasoning.

SALAD

~ Boil the potatoes, using 30g salt for each 2 litres water, then cool in the water. Cut into 2–3cm chunks, then mix in the remaining ingredients. Check the seasoning.

ASSEMBLE

~ Grill the bacon until crisp. Reheat the soup and serve in warmed bowls.

~ Separately serve the fish, bacon and potato salad.

COD BRANDADE WITH PICKLED VEGETABLES & GARLIC CROUTONS

Salt cod and brandade dishes are a staple of the Mediterranean. The salting process was traditionally heavy, though in this recipe it is incomparably lighter. It gives the cod a fullness of flavour and meatiness, but you don't taste the salt. Brandade is brilliant with bread and pickles. Here it is served as a light lunch, but you could easily just serve it on grilled bread, topped with canned piquillo peppers or a scattering of capers for something more robust.

Bake the potatoes while the cod is salting, to save time.

SALTED COD

500g cod fillet (thinner tail pieces are fine here), skinned and pin-boned

4 tablespoons coarse sea salt

2 tablespoons caster sugar

4 basil sprigs, bruised

finely grated zest of ½ lemon

2 tablespoons extra virgin olive oil

BRANDADE

2 large baking potatoes

8 tablespoons whole milk

juice of ¼ lemon

1 garlic clove, finely grated

320g cooked Salted cod, drained weight (see above and right)

6 tablespoons extra virgin olive oil

8 tablespoons vegetable oil

CROUTONS

2 slices of focaccia or other white bread, ripped into roughly 2cm pieces

4 tablespoons extra virgin olive oil

1 tablespoon chopped rosemary needles

½ garlic clove, crushed

PICKLED VEGETABLES

150g white wine vinegar

1 tablespoon caster sugar

2 teaspoons fine sea salt

1 carrot

1 yellow courgette

1 red onion, cut into segments (or Pickled onions, see page 304)

ASSEMBLE

16 artichoke hearts in olive oil

½ x 225g can of piquillo peppers

16 black olives, Kalamata if possible, washed and halved

handful of basil leaves

handful of rocket leaves

fennel tops (optional)

SALTED COD

- ~ Marinate the cod with all the ingredients except the oil for 1 hour.
- ~ Wash the fish, removing the zest and basil, and pat dry with kitchen paper.
- ~ Preheat the oven to 120°C.
- ~ Seal the fish in a foil pouch with the oil and bake until just cooked, about 20 minutes. Remove from the oven.

BRANDADE

- ~ Increase the oven temperature to 180°C and bake the potatoes until completely cooked through, soft and fluffy within. Cut in half, scoop out the insides, then push them through a sieve into a bowl.
- ~ Mix in the milk, lemon juice and garlic, then beat in half the cod vigorously to break it down.
- ~ Mix in the oils in a gradual stream to emulsify, beating hard.
- ~ Fold in the remaining cod, being careful not to break it up too much.

CROUTONS

- ~ Preheat the oven to 160°C.
- ~ Mix the focaccia and the oil, rosemary and garlic and spread out on a baking tray in a single layer.
- ~ Bake for 10 minutes, or until light golden. Drain on kitchen paper.

PICKLED VEGETABLES

- ~ Bring 450g water, the vinegar, sugar and salt to the boil in a saucepan, then remove from the heat.
- ~ Slice the carrot and courgette finely on a mandolin and store in a shallow bowl of some of the pickle liquor for at least 1 hour.
- ~ Blanch the red onion, if using, in simmering lightly salted water until just al dente, about 5 minutes, then lift with a slotted spoon into the bowl of carrot and courgette. Add the remaining pickle liquor and leave to cool.

ASSEMBLE

- ~ Spoon the brandade into bowls, then scatter over the rosemary-infused croutons, pickled and canned vegetables, olives, herbs and leaves, strewing with fennel tops, if you like.

ONE-HOUR CURED SALMON

This is a very simple recipe both to make and to remember. The taste is clean and fresh. It is a fantastic preparation whereby the reward far outweighs the labour; it genuinely feels like cheating! Add grated beetroot to the cure to stain the fish purple, if you like. Use the best possible salmon, and eat it on the day you cure it, or the next day. Any leftovers can be frozen to be used up later in fishcakes or a pie.

SALMON

½ fillet salmon (½ side of salmon), skinned and pin-boned

25g fine sea salt

25g caster sugar

25g lemon zest, finely pared, plus finely grated zest of 1 lemon and lemon wedges

25g dill, bruised, plus ½ bunch, roughly chopped, to serve

sliced rye bread, to serve

HORSERADISH & MOLASSES YOGURT

10g Dijon mustard

10g wholegrain mustard

20g muscovado sugar

1 teaspoon black treacle or molasses

juice of ½ lemon

2cm length of horseradish, peeled and finely grated

400g Greek yogurt

SALMON

~ Season the fish all over with the salt and sugar, then scatter both sides with the 25g each of pared lemon zest and dill. Cover with cling film and leave for 1 hour to cure in the refrigerator.

~ Fill the sink with plenty of cold water and wash the salmon in this. (If there is not enough water, you will simply be washing it in the brine, as opposed to removing it.)

~ Drain well on a new J-cloth for at least 4 hours, then roll in the roughly chopped dill and grated lemon zest.

~ Slice finely on an angle and place on a big platter, or divide among plates.

HORSERADISH & MOLASSES YOGURT

~ Whisk together all the ingredients, except the yogurt, with a pinch of salt, place in a saucepan and warm just enough to dissolve the sugar. Whisk into the yogurt.

~ Place in a new J-cloth, bring up the sides to form a bag, then place in a sieve over a bowl. Chill until thickened: about 2 hours. Transfer to a bowl.

TO SERVE

~ Serve the salmon with the yogurt sauce, plenty of rye bread and lemon wedges.

SEARED TUNA, CRUSHED AVOCADO & A TOASTED SESAME DRESSING

Tuna steak makes an easy dinner, though it's true that you pay for the convenience.

Dashi vinegar should be in your larder: it has an incredible savoury depth of flavour.

AVOCADO

2 ripe Haas avocados

finely grated zest and juice of 1 lime

½ bunch of coriander, chopped

fine sea salt

ROAST ONIONS

2 red onions

vegetable oil

DRESSING

50g light soy sauce

75g virgin rapeseed oil

1 teaspoon white miso paste

2 tablespoons caster sugar

2 tablespoons dashi vinegar (optional)

3 tablespoons toasted sesame seeds (see page 19)

2.5cm root ginger, peeled and grated

TUNA

4 x 150g tuna steaks

2 tablespoons vegetable oil

½ bunch chives, finely chopped

AVOCADO

~ Crush the avocados with 2 forks, then mix in all the remaining ingredients.

~ Keep in a container topped with cling film to prevent discolouration.

ROAST ONIONS

~ Preheat the oven to 160°C. Peel the onions and halve through the cores. Season on both sides, then colour in the oil in a hot ovenproof frying pan until deep golden.

~ Cover with foil and roast until tender, 20–25 minutes.

DRESSING

~ Mix all the ingredients in a saucepan with 1 tablespoon water, bring to the boil, then set aside.

TUNA

~ Bring the tuna out of the refrigerator 1 hour before serving. Heat a frying pan until smoking and salt the tuna well on both sides.

~ Colour the tuna in the oil for 30 seconds on each side. Place on a warm plate, cover and rest for 2 minutes.

TO SERVE

~ Serve the tuna, avocados, onions and chives, then spoon some dressing over the fish, offering the rest on the side.

BOURRIDE OF MONKFISH & MUSSELS WITH SAFFRON & FENNEL

Though this looks like a lot of work on paper, it is really quite simple and quick to prepare. That said, this is definitely a weekend affair rather than a school-night supper. Bourride in its most basic form is a Mediterranean fish stew, made with oily fish; the bones form a stock that is used to poach the fish and it is served with pungent garlic mayonnaise. This version is more velvety and indulgent, while keeping the briny acidity that makes a bourride so moreish.

Ask the fishmonger to remove the skin and membrane from the monkfish; other than that, there is very little preparation needed. Serve with crusty bread and chilled, crisp wine.

Serves 6–8

MUSSELS

250g white wine

1kg mussels, de-bearded and washed

GARLIC MAYONNAISE

3 egg yolks

2 large garlic cloves, minced

1 teaspoon Dijon mustard

juice of ½ lemon

2 tablespoons Chardonnay vinegar

large pinch of fine sea salt

small pinch of caster sugar

250g vegetable oil

150g extra virgin olive oil

BOURRIDE

½ white or brown onion, peeled and core removed, cut into segments

½ fennel bulb, finely sliced

2 celery sticks, peeled of string and sliced 2cm thick on the diagonal

1 leek, halved, washed and sliced 2cm thick on the diagonal

50g extra virgin olive oil

pinch of saffron threads

4 pared strips of orange zest

2 star anise

150ml white vermouth

100g double cream

8 cooked new potatoes, halved

8 artichoke hearts in oil, halved

500g finger-length monkfish goujons, lightly seasoned with salt

4 handfuls of baby spinach, washed

200g green beans, blanched for 3 minutes in boiling salted water (see page 162), then refreshed in iced water and drained

1 tablespoon chopped thyme leaves

handful of fennel tops

fine sea salt

warm baguette, to serve

MUSSELS

~ Bring the wine and 250g water to the boil in a large saucepan, then add the mussels and cover with a lid.

~ Cook over a high heat for 3 minutes until they open and are just cooked. Discard any that remain closed.

~ Pour through a colander to keep the stock, then pick out the meat from the shells, keeping 12 mussels in the shells for presentation.

~ Strain the juice through a double layer of new J-cloth or muslin and keep the picked mussels in a small amount of their liquor, just to keep them moist.

GARLIC MAYONNAISE

~ Place all the ingredients for the mayonnaise, except the oils, in a container with 1 tablespoon water and blend with a hand blender.

~ Blend in the oils gradually until thick and homogenous. Check the seasoning and keep chilled.

BOURRIDE

~ Sweat the onion, fennel, celery and leek in the olive oil with a pinch of salt, the saffron, orange zest and star anise, covering with a lid. Cook for about 5 minutes, until softened but not completely cooked.

~ Add the vermouth and boil for 10 seconds, then add the reserved, strained mussel stock and the cream and return to a gentle simmer. Cook for 5 minutes, then check the vegetables are tender; if they are, remove the orange zest and star anise.

~ Pour some of the hot broth from the pan into a jug, then whisk this into 300g of the garlic mayonnaise. Now return the mayonnaise mixture to the saucepan and mix with the remaining liquor to combine. Cook over a low heat, stirring, until the sauce thickens.

~ Add the potatoes and artichokes, then the monkfish, and poach gently for 3 minutes until just cooked.

~ Next, carefully mix in the spinach to wilt, then add the cooked green beans, chopped thyme and mussels, both those in the shell and out.

~ Scatter over the fennel tops and serve immediately, with warm baguette, offering any of the remaining garlic mayonnaise on the side.

CHARRED MACKEREL WITH FREEKEH TABBOULEH

The combination of smoky, oily fish and sharp, herbaceous salad is so good it feels pre-ordained. Mackerel is plentiful, cheap and delicious and, when fresh, one of the purest and cleanest tastes of the sea you will ever encounter. The freekeh adds a delicious bite, though bulgur is absolutely fine to use as well.

FREEKEH

150g freekeh

1 teaspoon fine sea salt

TABBOULEH

400g ripe tomatoes, finely chopped

100g cucumber, finely chopped

90g parsley, finely chopped

30g mint leaves, finely chopped

5 spring onions, finely sliced

100g pomegranate seeds

finely grated zest and juice of 1 lemon

5 tablespoons extra virgin olive oil

1 teaspoon fine sea salt

1 teaspoon ground cumin

MACKEREL

4 mackerel, butterflied or filleted

4 tablespoons extra virgin olive oil

4 tablespoons Lemon dressing (see page 294)

pinch of sea salt flakes

FREEKEH

153

~ Put the freekeh and salt in a saucepan with 1 litre water, bring to the boil, then simmer for 12 minutes. Drain well, then spread on a tray to air-dry.

TABBOULEH

~ Season the tomatoes and cucumber with a pinch of fine sea salt and leave for at least 15 minutes while you prepare the rest of the ingredients. Drain off the excess liquid and mix with the freekeh, herbs, spring onions and pomegranate seeds.

~ In a separate bowl, mix together the lemon zest and juice, oil, salt and cumin, then stir this through the tabbouleh. Check the seasoning.

MACKEREL

~ Brush the fish with the oil and season well on both sides with fine sea salt.

~ Heat a chargrill pan until smoking, add the fish skin-side down and cook until blackened. Flip over to lightly seal the flesh side. The whole process should take no more than a minute.

~ Transfer to a tray and drizzle with the lemon dressing and sea salt flakes.

TO SERVE

~ Spoon the tabbouleh on to a serving dish and place the mackerel on top.

CRISPY COD WITH CUCUMBER, LOVAGE & SPRING ONION

Posh fried fish, though this is actually light and healthy rather than greasy. By salting the cod, the flesh is firmed significantly. You need to start the batter a day before you need it.

BATTER

1 teaspoon fast-action dried yeast

175g plain flour

pinch of caster sugar

pinch of fine sea salt

SAUCE

150g Greek yogurt

150g Mayonnaise (see page 294)

1 shot of gin

2 tablespoons Chardonnay vinegar

2 tablespoons chopped lovage or parsley

2 spring onions, sliced on an angle

¼ cucumber, peeled, deseeded and finely chopped

finely grated zest and juice of ½ lemon, plus lemon wedges to serve

COD

4 x 120g meaty neck-end cod fillets, skinned and pin-boned

4 tablespoons coarse sea salt

ASSEMBLE

vegetable oil, for deep-frying

cornflour, to coat

BATTER

~ Dissolve the yeast in 250g warm water, then mix into the dry ingredients in a large bowl.

~ Leave to ferment at room temperature for 1 hour, then chill for 24 hours.

~ Pour off the water that will have risen to the surface. It's now ready to use.

SAUCE

~ Mix everything together, check the seasoning, then put into small bowls.

COD

~ Season the cod heavily with the salt, set aside for 15 minutes, then wash off and pat dry on kitchen paper.

ASSEMBLE

~ Heat a large pan of oil to 180°C, making sure the oil comes no more than one-third of the way up the sides of the pan.

~ Dip the cod pieces in cornflour, then dust off the excess.

~ Dip into the batter, drain off the excess, then deep-fry in the hot oil for 4–5 minutes.

~ Remove with a slotted spoon and drain on kitchen paper.

~ Place on plates and serve with lemon wedges and the sauce on the side.

SMOKED HADDOCK
BUBBLE & SQUEAK &
WARM MUSTARD DRESSING

Here we are using flaked smoked haddock in the bubble and squeak, but you could just as well add smoked ham hock, pancetta or another smoked oily fish (don't use salmon though, which would overcook).

There are a few key things to get right when poaching eggs. First, use the freshest eggs: when you crack open a properly fresh egg, it will hold its shape on a plate and there will be a clear outline of viscous white. This means, as you crack a fresh egg into a pan to poach, the white will stay close to the yolk and envelop it, rather than dissipate into the water. Using a deep saucepan increases the 'drop-time' of the egg before it hits the bottom. So if the pan is deep and the water boiling, the white should start to cook as it drops, forming that desirable teardrop shape. Finally, once the eggs have been cracked, reduce the heat so there are no bubbles to agitate the eggs and potentially break up the whites.

All common sense, but not necessarily obvious if you haven't thought about it... or poached thousands of eggs over the course of your career!

BUBBLE & SQUEAK

500g (about 2) Maris Piper baking potatoes

200g smoked haddock fillet

250g Hispi cabbage, shredded

25g salted butter, plus more to fry

1 garlic clove, crushed

plain flour, to dust

fine sea salt

DRESSING

120g extra thick double cream, or to taste

30g red wine vinegar

60g virgin rapeseed oil

1 tablespoon chopped chives

1 tablespoon chopped parsley leaves

1 teaspoon Dijon mustard

1 teaspoon wholegrain mustard

1 teaspoon caster sugar, or to taste

POACHED EGGS

white wine vinegar

4 eggs

black pepper

BUBBLE & SQUEAK

- Microwave the potatoes at 900W (on high) for 10 minutes, or however long it takes in your microwave until completely cooked. (You could equally well bake them, if you prefer.) Scoop out the middles: you should have about 250g cooked potato.
- Steam the smoked haddock over boiling water until just cooked, then leave to cool slightly and flake the fish, removing any bones.
- Cook the Hispi cabbage in the 25g butter with the garlic until just wilted, about 3 minutes, then transfer to a tray to arrest the cooking.
- Lightly season the cooked potato, then mix in the cabbage, followed by the smoked haddock flakes. Check the seasoning and adjust if necessary.
- Using your hands or a ring, make patties of the bubble and squeak, then dust well in plain flour.
- Heat a medium frying pan, add some butter and cook until it starts to foam, then add the patties and fry on both sides until crusted and golden brown.

DRESSING

- Whisk everything together with a pinch of salt to combine, then check the seasoning and acidity. If you find it too acidic – though remember it does need to be sharp to balance the finished dish – add a splash of cream and a sprinkling of sugar.
- Set over a low heat and keep warm while you poach the eggs.

POACHED EGGS

- Bring a deep saucepan of water to the boil. Add a healthy splash of white wine vinegar and 1 tablespoon salt for each litre of water.
- Crack in the eggs, then reduce the heat under the pan so the water is only gently bubbling.
- Poach the eggs for about 3 minutes, until set on the outside, with warm liquid yolks within. Remove with a slotted spoon on to kitchen paper and season lightly with salt and black pepper.

TO SERVE

- Divide the bubble and squeak between warmed plates, then top with the eggs and spoon over the warm dressing.

STEAMED LEMON SOLE, CRAB MAYONNAISE, COURGETTE & CAPERS

Lemon sole is one of the smaller flat fish, so try to find the biggest available, or the fillets may feel rather diminutive. This dish oozes restaurant quality, but has very few ingredients and is simple to put together. I know it's a bit retro and tongue-in-cheek with the courgette scales, but it will raise a smile.

CRAB MAYONNAISE

240g white and brown crab, picked
100g Mayonnaise (see page 294)
40g Greek yogurt
1 tablespoon chopped parsley leaves
fine sea salt

CRISPY CAPERS

2–4 tablespoons vegetable oil
2 tablespoons olive oil (optional)
4 tablespoons capers, washed and dried

COURGETTE

2 yellow courgettes
250g pickle liquor (see page 304)

SOLE

2 lemon sole, filleted and skinned

ASSEMBLE

150g samphire, picked
1 tablespoon unsalted butter
finely grated zest of 1 lemon

CRAB MAYONNAISE

~ Mix everything together with a pinch of salt and keep chilled.

CRISPY CAPERS

~ I use 2 types of oil as olive oil alone may be too bitter, but use all vegetable oil if you prefer. Heat the oil in a pan until hot, then add the capers and fry for 1 minute until crisp. Drain well on kitchen paper.

COURGETTE

~ Slice the courgettes finely into rounds 2–3mm thick on a mandolin and store in the pickle liquor for 30 minutes.

SOLE

~ Lightly season the fish with salt and top with overlapping slices of the pickled courgette to resemble scales.
~ Place in a steamer basket and steam for 5 minutes, or until just cooked. If you don't have a steamer big enough, bake in a baking tray in a gentle oven, topped with foil to trap the steam.

ASSEMBLE

~ Blanch the samphire for 30 seconds in boiling water to wilt, then drain and toss with the butter. Keep warm.
~ Serve the fish with the capers, lemon zest, samphire and crab mayonnaise.

ROAST SKATE WITH SPICED MUSSELS, CRISPY ONIONS & CURRY LEAVES

This dish takes a bit more preparation than some of the others in this book, but all the stages are quite quick and the biggest job is making a mussel broth. This is a pleasure to cook and deeply satisfying to eat.

Skate is a forgiving fish: whereas some fish can overcook very quickly, skate stays tender and juicy for longer due to its high collagen content, and is often best when exposed to a very hot oven. You don't have to cook it in the chargrill pan first, but it does add a nice depth of flavour.

RAISINS

1 jasmine teabag

50g golden raisins

MUSSELS

250g white wine

600g mussels, de-bearded and washed

SPICED BROTH

200g Spanish onions, finely sliced

20g fresh root ginger, peeled and sliced

4 tablespoons virgin rapeseed oil

½ teaspoon curry powder

½ teaspoon ground turmeric

300g double cream

juice of ½ lemon

fine sea salt

CRISPY GARNISHES

vegetable oil, for deep-frying

1 white onion

gram flour, to dust

1 quantity Batter (see page 155), optional

1 teaspoon coriander seeds, toasted (see page 19) and crushed

1 teaspoon ground cumin

2 large handfuls of fresh curry leaves

SKATE

2 medium skate wings, on the bone

virgin rapeseed oil

25g salted butter, melted

ASSEMBLE

250g green beans, stems removed

2 tablespoons chopped coriander leaves

————

RAISINS

- Bring 250g water to the boil, add the teabag and pour over the raisins in a bowl. Leave to soak for 1 hour.

MUSSELS

~ Pour the wine and 250g water into a large saucepan and bring to the boil, then add the mussels and cover.

- Cook over a high heat for 3 minutes until they open and are just cooked. Discard any that remain closed.
- Pour through a colander, reserving the stock, then pick the meat from the shells, keeping 8 in the shells.
- Strain the stock through a double layer of new J-cloth or muslin and keep the picked mussels in a small amount of their liquor, to keep moist.

SPICED BROTH

- In a saucepan over a gentle heat, sweat the onions and ginger with a pinch of salt in the rapeseed oil for 10 minutes.
- Add the curry powder and turmeric and cook for 5 minutes over low heat.
- Add the reserved, strained mussel stock and cream and reduce by half.
- Add 200g of the picked mussels and cook for 1 minute, then add the lemon juice and blend until smooth.

CRISPY GARNISHES

- Heat the oil in a large saucepan to 180°C, being sure it only fills one-third of the pan.
- Carefully peel the onion, keeping the root intact, then cut into thin wedges, going through the root each time.
- Dip the wedges in lightly seasoned gram flour, then into the batter, if using.

- Deep-fry until light golden and crispy, then place on kitchen paper to blot off excess oil. Dust with the coriander and cumin.
- Deep-fry the curry leaves in the same oil for 10 seconds, or until they stop bubbling. Drain well on kitchen paper, then season lightly with salt.

SKATE

- Preheat the oven to 220°C.
- Cut each skate wing into 2 x 200g pieces and bring to room temperature before cooking. Season on both sides and brush with the rapeseed oil.
- Colour in a hot chargrill pan on both sides until well coloured.
- Transfer to a roasting tray and brush with the melted butter. Roast for about 8 minutes until just cooked, then remove, top loosely with foil and leave to rest for 5 minutes.

ASSEMBLE

- Blanch the beans for 3 minutes in boiling salted water (use 20g salt for each litre of water), then drain. Place in warmed bowls with the skate.
- Gently reheat the broth, then add the remaining cooked mussels, in and out of the shell, drained raisins and herbs, and spoon over the skate.
- Scatter over the crispy onions and curry leaves.

PLAICE ON THE BONE WITH WARM TARTARE SAUCE

Cooking plaice this way keeps the fish moist, makes a stock, then crisps the skin at the end.

Do use a probe thermometer when cooking whole fish; it should reach 50°C at the core to be just cooked. Cooking new potatoes this way works brilliantly: it's hard going back to simply boiled once you've tasted these.

NEW POTATOES

500g Jersey Royals or Charlotte potatoes, washed, halved if large

100g salted butter, chopped

100g unsalted butter, chopped

BROCCOLI

250g purple-sprouting broccoli, or other tender broccoli stalks, trimmed

25g salted butter

fine sea salt

PLAICE

1 x 2kg whole plaice

250g white wine

drizzle of extra virgin olive oil

150g Mayonnaise (see page 294)

2 spring onions, sliced on an angle

1 tablespoon chopped gherkins

1 tablespoon chopped capers

2 tablespoons chopped parsley leaves

pinch of sea salt flakes

NEW POTATOES

~ Preheat the oven to 160°C.

~ Seal the potatoes and butters in a pouch made from 2 lengths of criss-crossed foil. (I use salted and unsalted butter here to achieve the correct level of seasoning.) Cook for 1 hour.

BROCCOLI

~ Blanch the broccoli for 3 minutes in boiling salted water (use 20g salt for each litre of water) until just tender, then drain well and toss in the butter.

PLAICE

~ Preheat the oven to 160°C.

~ Season the plaice all over with salt and place in a tray with the wine and 250g water. Seal with foil and bake for 20 minutes. Remove from the oven. Preheat the grill to its highest setting.

~ Pour off and reserve the liquor.

~ Drizzle the fish lightly with oil and place under the grill to crisp the skin.

~ Place the fish liquor and mayonnaise in a saucepan, bring to a simmer, then remove from the heat and add the remaining ingredients.

TO SERVE

~ Sprinkle the fish with sea salt flakes. Serve with the vegetables and sauce.

FISH

BAKED SALMON,
BEURRE BLANC,
RYE & ASPARAGUS

Salmon is often fried or roasted, but such aggressive cooking can result in something quite dry if your timings are just slightly out. Here it is gently baked to showcase the buttery flesh. It is also briefly cured beforehand to firm it up and give an engrained seasoning, though if you are short of time, this step can be omitted and you can simply season the fish with fine sea salt before cooking.

I should probably not call this sauce a beurre blanc, as it is so far from the classic recipe, and yet I find it far more palatable than the intensely fatty and acidic original, more aligned with today's eating habits, far more mellow and well balanced.

The addition of rosemary is not compulsory, but it does add its savouriness to the sauce. The rye crumb here soaks up the sauce and becomes a delicious malty 'porridge' as it rehydrates.

You can make this dish with 4 salmon fillets instead, in which case cure them for just 15 minutes and bake for another 15 minutes.

BEURRE BLANC

60g banana shallots, finely sliced

25g white wine vinegar

75g white wine

100g whipping cream

250g salted butter, melted

juice of ¼ lemon

1 teaspoon Chardonnay vinegar

2 rosemary sprigs

RYE CRUMB

4 slices of pumpernickel or rye bread

ASPARAGUS

16 green asparagus spears

2 tablespoons shop-bought garlic oil

2 tablespoons Lemon dressing
(see page 294)

fine sea salt

sea salt flakes

SALMON

600g One-hour cured salmon
(see page 144), rinsed and drained,
but not rolled in dill and lemon zest

4 tablespoons shop-bought garlic oil

2 basil sprigs, bruised

BEURRE BLANC

~ Place the shallots, white wine vinegar
and wine in a saucepan and set
over a low heat until it has reduced
completely. It should still be moist,
but with no visible liquid.

~ Add 100g water and the cream and
bring to the boil.

~ Blend in a blender, then add the
melted butter in a steady stream, still
blending, until emulsified.

~ Once emulsified, add the lemon juice
and Chardonnay vinegar and transfer
to a bowl.

~ Add the rosemary sprigs to infuse
for 5 minutes, then pass the sauce
through a sieve into a clean saucepan.

RYE CRUMB

~ Blitz the bread in a food processor to
coarse crumbs.

ASPARAGUS

~ Preheat a chargrill pan until smoky.

~ Snap off the woody bases from the
asparagus spears, then trim them to
neaten. Remove the 'thistles' – the
leaflets that protrude from the stems –
but do not peel.

~ Dress with the garlic oil and season
with fine salt, then place in the pan
and toast on all sides until smoky but
still al dente: 3–4 minutes.

~ Remove and transfer to a tray to arrest
the cooking. Dress lightly with lemon
dressing, then season with salt flakes.

SALMON

~ Preheat the oven to 140°C.

~ Criss-cross 2 foil sheets and place the
salmon in the centre, then top with
the oil and basil and wrap to seal.

~ Bake for about 25 minutes until just
cooked. Remove from the oven and
leave to rest for 5 minutes. Divide into
4 rustic-looking pieces.

TO SERVE

~ Spoon the rye crumb into 4 warmed,
deep plates, then add the salmon and
asparagus spears.

~ Serve with a jug of the hot beurre
blanc for guests to help themselves.

BRAISED TURBOT WITH LEMON VERBENA

Feel free to use any other flat fish here, such as halibut or brill. This recipe is included in this chapter's collection because it is a great skill to be able to fillet a fish and make a delicious sauce from the bones that is then used to poach the fillets.

This sauce is a great example of how you can achieve restaurant finesse at home, as layers of seasoning are added as you make it. The bones are chopped small to maximise their surface area and minimise their cooking time, resulting in a fresher, more flavoursome sauce. The wine is boiled to remove some of its acidity, but the vermouth is added raw to keep its fragrance. It is all these points of attention to detail that normally separate the professional kitchen from the domestic... until now.

Incidentally, if you don't disturb the neighbours when bruising the lemon grass, you are not bashing it hard enough!

I serve this with a simple cucumber and samphire salad and new potatoes.

TURBOT

1 x 2kg turbot

SAUCE

1 large banana shallot, finely sliced (100g prepared weight)

2 tablespoons olive oil

250g button mushrooms, finely sliced (must be white and firm, not grey)

juice of ½ lemon

175g white wine

175g vermouth

3 lemon grass stalks, bruised and finely chopped

175g whole milk

175g double cream

1 teaspoon cornflour

4 lemon verbena sprigs

fine sea salt

ASSEMBLE

lemon verbena tips and chive flowers (optional)

TURBOT

- Take the head off the fish using a sharp or serrated knife. Set it aside.
- Cut down either side of the main backbone until you reach the bones, then cut across, using the bones as a guide, to remove both fillets.
- Turn the fish and repeat on the other side, then skin all 4 fillets and keep in the refrigerator until needed.
- Chop the fish bones and head into small pieces and wash under cold running water for 5 minutes, then drain well in a colander.

SAUCE

- Sweat the shallot and a pinch of salt in the oil, in a medium covered saucepan over a gentle heat, for 10 minutes, or until soft.
- Add the mushrooms, a pinch of salt and the lemon juice. Mix and sweat for 5 minutes to release the juices.
- Season the turbot bones with another pinch of salt. Add to the pan, cover and sweat for another 5 minutes.
- In a separate pan, bring the wine to the boil, then remove it from the heat.
- Add the wine to the pan with the turbot bones. Briefly boil again for 30 seconds, then pour in the vermouth and return to the boil.

- Add the lemon grass, milk and cream. Return to the boil for a final time and simmer gently for 10 minutes.
- Pass through a sieve, squeezing hard to push as much of the fish and aromats as possible into the sauce, then return to a clean saucepan.
- Whisk the cornflour in a cup with enough water to make a paste, then add it to the sauce over a medium-high heat and cook until it returns to the boil and thickens.
- Add the lemon verbena, allow it to infuse for 2 minutes off the heat, then pass through a sieve once more, this time not pushing it through.

ASSEMBLE

- Preheat the oven to 140°C.
- Pour the still-warm sauce into a baking dish and add the fish fillets.
- Cover with foil and bake until just cooked, 10–15 minutes. If you have a probe thermometer, the fish should reach 46–50°C at the core.
- Divide between warmed bowls, or arrange on a large warmed platter, and serve immediately, with lemon verbena tips and chive flowers, if using.

GRILLED BREAM WITH PINK GRAPEFRUIT, HONEY & FENNEL

Gilthead bream is one of the best-quality farmed fish you can buy. It is always consistent in quality and very good value; not as meaty as sea bass, but with lovely oily flesh and crisp skin. It is great cooked over the barbecue or under a hot grill.

This dressing is as delicious as it is simple. Feel free to chop and change as you wish: lemon and mint would work brilliantly, as would blood orange and sage.

DRESSING

2 pink grapefruits, segmented (see page 69), with 6 tablespoons of their juice

6 tablespoons extra virgin olive oil

1 tablespoon Chardonnay vinegar

1 tablespoon clear honey

1 tablespoon thyme leaves

1 tablespoon coriander seeds, toasted (see page 19) and crushed

BREAM & FENNEL

2 fennel bulbs

1 teaspoon fennel seeds

100ml white vermouth

2 gilthead bream, scaled, filleted and pin-boned by your fishmonger

4 tablespoons extra virgin olive oil

fine sea salt

DRESSING

- Mix everything together and warm through in a pan. Do not heat it too much, or the grapefruit segments will cook and collapse.

BREAM & FENNEL

~ Preheat the grill to its highest setting.

~ Slice the fennel lengthways as finely as possible on a mandolin or with a sharp knife, then mix in a roasting tray with the fennel seeds and vermouth. Season lightly with salt.

~ Lightly season the fish on both sides with fine salt, then place skin-side up on top of the fennel, to cover the bulk of it. Spoon 1 tablespoon of the oil over each fish fillet

~ Grill under the preheated grill for about 8 minutes, until the fennel has wilted but the fish is cooked through and has a crispy skin.

TO SERVE

~ Divide the fennel and fish between 4 warmed bowls and spoon around the warm grapefruit dressing.

MEAT

The best home-cooked meat dishes are intrinsically comforting and positively rustic. Somehow, a certain lack of aesthetic refinement gives the eater the reassurance that they will taste amazing and satisfy profoundly. We don't want meat to look pretty; we want it to be honest, carnal and plentiful. Making pies, dumplings and toad-in-the-hole is perhaps old-fashioned, but these are classics for good reason: they are simple to prepare and well worth the effort.

When you eat meat, an animal has given its life. This is something that we don't always take time to consider, but it's important not to take meat for granted, given the ease with which we can obtain it these days. What was once a luxury has now become commonplace.

Intensively reared meat has so many negatives: it is not delicious, it provides little nourishment, the animals may have been treated inhumanely and its production causes huge collateral damage to the environment. It is only collectively as consumers that we can have an impact, and buying cheap meat only endorses intensive rearing and enables its continued production. It is far better to eat less but better quality meat. You really will notice the difference, both when you cook it and when you eat it.

I think it would be useful to give a few words of basic science here, before you attempt these dishes, to hopefully remove some of the mystique around cooking with meat, get rid of any guesswork and help you to achieve results you are consistently happy with.

ROOM TEMPERATURE

Before cooking meat, always bring it to room temperature. The importance of this is hard to overstate. Assume your refrigerator is set to 3°C, the kitchen is at 20°C and you want to cook a piece of meat to 55°C (medium-rare). The sole act of bringing the meat to room temperature will account for a raise in its core temperature of 17°C, which is about one-third of the total cooking needed!

SEASON

Season tender cuts such as fillets and loins with fine salt just before cooking. Larger cuts, such as the rack of rose veal in this chapter, often benefit from a brief cure or brine, so the seasoning can permeate right through. As a rule, meat can take a heavier hand than fish when salting, but the level required depends on the overall thickness and weight of the cut.

COOKING DEGREE

Meat is made up of lots of protein strands that, when raw, are flaccid and straight (the reason why you can fold a raw steak over itself). But as meat is cooked, these strands coil, interlink and tighten (so well-done steak is stiff).

When cooking meat, you want the protein to cook to just the right degree so the meat is tender and juicy. I find the often-repeated method of comparing the feel of meat to different parts of the palm of your hand utterly confusing and unhelpful. Determining the *cuisson* (cooking degree) of any cut of meat is a skill that comes with experience, but using a probe thermometer removes any guesswork and doubt (as long as meat is well rested, there is no harm in using a probe; if it's a thinner piece of meat, just go in at an acute angle to maximise the surface area of the needle in contact with the meat).

The cooking degrees for red meat are very straightforward: 50°C core temperature is rare; 55°C is medium-rare; 60°C is medium; 65°C is medium-well; 70°C and above is well-done. Fillet steak is best cooked closer to rare, as it is so tender, whereas meats such as lamb and duck need to be firmer and cooked to at least 55°C before resting. For chicken breast or tender pork cuts, 64°C is about right. For any hard-working muscles such as legs, shoulders or belly, the cooking time should be much longer. The core temperature needs to not only reach 70°C, but to maintain that over some time to tenderise the meat. By cooking larger, tougher joints of meat slowly, their protein strands coagulate more gently and fewer juices are lost,

so the meat stays moister. By cooking it quickly, the protein can tighten fast and cause a lot of juice to be lost; while this is great for gravy, you ultimately want to keep the juices in the meat, not lose them to the pan.

REST

More experienced cooks would always rest meat, but not for nearly long enough, in my opinion. Essentially, when meat comes out of a hot oven, its protein strands are very tight as they are undergoing the cooking process: think of them as if they were a tensed muscle after a workout. The resting process is the relaxation of these protein strands into something less rigid, and therefore more tender.

The bigger the piece of meat and the hotter the oven, the longer the resting period needed. A steak needs about a 10-minute rest; a large rib of beef or whole roast chicken closer to an hour, if the oven was hot. I bet that's much longer than you thought. As a simple rule of thumb, allow the same resting time as cooking time, capping it at about an hour. Rest meat somewhere warm, or just cover it loosely with foil to trap the heat without causing steam. If you carve meat that hasn't been rested, the juices will flood out and any nice pink colour in red meat will be lost along with them.

COLD ROAST BEEF ON TOAST, WARM HORSERADISH BUTTERMILK

The real satisfaction of this is in its textures: thin-sliced beef, pillowy focaccia and a tangle of leaves, all brought together by warm buttermilk. The sauce has a lovely acidity and heat and is also delicious with baked salmon.

BEEF

500g beef sirloin, trimmed

garlic oil (shop-bought)

rosemary

fine sea salt

BUTTERMILK

250g whole milk

50g buttermilk

1 tablespoon cornflour

125g warm, melted unsalted butter

1 garlic clove, finely chopped

30g horseradish, finely grated

juice of ½ lemon

ASSEMBLE

4 large slices of focaccia

4 tablespoons garlic oil

4 handfuls of watercress or rocket

1 tablespoon sliced cornichons

1 tablespoon capers, washed and drained

handful of tarragon leaves

¼ red onion, finely sliced and rinsed

4 tablespoons Lemon dressing
(see page 294)

BEEF

~ Preheat the oven to 130°C.

~ Season the beef all over with salt, then colour all over in a hot chargrill pan with a little garlic oil.

~ Transfer to a roasting tray and roast until the core temperature reads 52°C; this should take about 20 minutes. Leave for 15 minutes on a warm plate, topped with foil, then rub with bruised rosemary. The core temperature should now be 55°C.

~ Cool to room temperature.

BUTTERMILK

~ Bring the milk and buttermilk to the boil. Don't worry about it splitting.

~ Whisk the cornflour and 3 tablespoons water, then whisk this into the milk. Return to the boil to thicken.

~ Blend in the butter, a pinch of salt, the garlic and horseradish, then leave for 5 minutes. Add the lemon juice and pass through a sieve. Keep warm.

ASSEMBLE

~ Toast the focaccia until golden, then drizzle with the garlic oil.

~ Toss the leaves, cornichons, capers, tarragon and onion with the dressing.

~ Sit the salad on the focaccia, then top with finely sliced roast beef. Serve the horseradish buttermilk on the side.

SAUSAGE ROLLS WITH PICCALILLI

I have made countless sausage rolls over the years. Whenever customers asked for canapé parties at my first restaurant, among the more esoteric options I would always like to offer these as a crowd-pleaser to soak up the alcohol. They were always the first things to be devoured, as were any trimmings or leftovers by the kitchen staff.

Makes 4 generous sausage rolls

FILLING

½ white onion, finely chopped

25g salted butter

8 sage leaves, finely chopped

leaves from 2 thyme sprigs, finely chopped

250g minced pork

250g sausagemeat

100g minced smoked streaky bacon

¼ teaspoon ground mace

1 tablespoon Dijon mustard

1 Braeburn apple, grated (avoid the core)

1 tablespoon Worcestershire sauce

3 slices of white bread, blended into breadcrumbs

1 teaspoon fine sea salt

½ teaspoon black pepper

ASSEMBLE

1 egg yolk

2 tablespoons cream (any type)

2 x 320g puff pastry sheets

1 tablespoon poppy seeds

Piccalilli (see page 295)

FILLING

~ Sweat the onion in the butter for 20 minutes until softened, add the herbs and pour on to a tray to cool.

~ Mix the cooled onion mix with all the remaining ingredients. Transfer to 2 large piping bags, or roll into 5cm-wide cylinders and wrap in greaseproof paper.

ASSEMBLE

~ Mix the yolk and cream together in a small bowl to make an egg wash.

~ Cut the tips off the piping bags; the sausagemeat should emerge 50 per cent thicker than an actual sausage.

~ Pipe the mix in a neat line all the way down each length of puff pastry about 5cm from the edge. If not using piping bags, transfer the sausage cylinders over to the pastry instead.

~ Roll the pastry over the filling, then trim it to leave about 1cm overlap. Push down lightly to seal, and make sure the seam is on the underside. You should get 2 sausage rolls from each length of puff pastry.

~ Repeat until all the sausage mix is used up. Cut into 15cm lengths, or however long you want them to be.

~ Transfer to baking trays lined with greaseproof paper, leaving a gap for the air to circulate.

~ Preheat the oven to 200°C.

~ Egg wash the sausage rolls well all over using a pastry brush, then leave for 15 minutes to dry, then repeat. This is key to their golden appearance.

~ Immediately after the second egg wash, score with a sharp knife and scatter lightly with poppy seeds.

~ Bake for 15 minutes, then reduce the oven temperature to 180°C and bake for another 15 minutes. Leave them to cool for about 15 minutes, then serve with a bowl of piccalilli.

CRISPY CHICKEN WINGS WITH SMOKED PAPRIKA

This recipe is an absolute winner. It tastes homely and moreish rather than greasy and bad for you. The flavours are quite complex, with the heat of the garlic, smokiness of the paprika, acidity of the vinegar, fragrance of the lemon and woodiness of the oregano. If chicken wings are too messy, feel free to use boneless thighs instead. Serve with a potato salad and some toasted sweetcorn. Coleslaw (see page 75) would be delicious alongside.

Serves 4–6

CHICKEN

400g buttermilk

100g whipping cream

1 teaspoon fine sea salt, plus 15g

1kg chicken wings, thighs or drumsticks

vegetable oil, for deep-frying

500g cornflour

dried oregano, to serve

SAUCE

100g olive oil

100g vegetable oil

20g garlic cloves, peeled

20g white wine vinegar

1 teaspoon fine sea salt

1 teaspoon smoked paprika

¼ teaspoon chilli powder

finely grated zest and juice of
½ lemon

CHICKEN

~ Mix the buttermilk and cream with 1 teaspoon salt, then leave the chicken in this overnight.

~ The next day, heat the oil in a large pan to 180°C.

~ Drain the chicken, keeping the buttermilk marinade.

~ Mix together the cornflour and 15g salt. Dip the wings in the cornflour, then dip back in the buttermilk and finally once again into the cornflour, to get a thick layer of coating.

~ Shake off the excess cornflour, then fry in the hot oil for 5 minutes for wings or thighs and 10 minutes for drumsticks. Do this in batches, to avoid overcrowding the pan.

~ Drain well, then place in a bowl and roll in plenty of the sauce. Finally, sprinkle generously with oregano.

SAUCE

~ Blend all the ingredients together in a blender, ensuring all the garlic has been puréed.

TO SERVE

~ Divide the chicken into serving bowls – or place on a large platter – and serve immediately, making sure to provide plenty of napkins.

GRILLED QUAIL WITH PISTACHIO, MINT & ORANGE BLOSSOM

Quail is delicious, but you are forced to work hard to get to the meat, given the diminutive size of the bird. I always think it is preferable to do this work in the kitchen rather than at the dining room table, as that makes it so much more enjoyable for your guests.

Baharat is a North African spice mix that is rounded and sweet through the inclusion of cloves, cinnamon and nutmeg. It is delicious with any grilled meat, but particularly with quail. It is hard to make a smaller amount, but it does keep well. The pistachio, mint and orange blossom dressing is fragrant, complex and moreish, but quick and easy to make.

Finally, a word on cooking the legs and breasts on a bird: do it separately, as the legs take far longer. You need two separate cooking methods to get the best results, rather than taking an umbrella approach that will unilaterally result in overcooked breasts or undercooked legs.

It is definitely worth grinding your own cinnamon for this or any other recipe. When this spice is commercially ground, it is also heat treated, a process which dulls the fragrance of its essential oils.

QUAIL

4 extra-large quail

fine sea salt

1 quantity Baharat (see page 295)

olive oil

PISTACHIO, MINT & ORANGE BLOSSOM SAUCE

1 tablespoon orange blossom water

finely grated zest and juice of ½ lemon

½ garlic clove, crushed

1 tablespoon clear honey

200g shelled unsalted pistachios

100g olive oil

50g vegetable oil

handful of finely chopped parsley leaves

handful of finely chopped mint leaves

pinch of fine sea salt

PICKLED CARROTS

250ml pickle liquor (see page 304)

1 tablespoon orange blossom water

1 bunch of baby carrots, peeled, any green tops trimmed

ASSEMBLE

1 Romaine lettuce, cut into wedges

1 bunch of radishes, washed and trimmed

4 tablespoons thick Greek yogurt

freshly ground black pepper

QUAIL

~ Preheat the oven to 150°C.

~ Take the legs and breasts off the bone of the birds, exactly as you would do with a chicken, just on a smaller scale. For the breasts, cut either side of the breastbones and use the wishbones as a guide as you bring the knife down and outwards. Cut inside each thigh between the thigh and the carcass, then pull down to detach the bone and cut through in between the shoulder joint to detach the whole leg from the body. Finally, remove the bone from the thigh by cutting either side of it and then underneath it, then cutting it off where it meets the bone going down to the drumstick. Repeat to joint all the quail.

~ Season the legs with salt and about ½ teaspoon baharat for each 2 legs and place the legs in a foil pouch with a drizzle of olive oil. Seal the pouches, then bake in the oven for 30 minutes.

~ Preheat the grill to its highest setting.

~ Season the breasts with salt and about ½ teaspoon baharat for each 2 breasts, then drizzle with some olive oil.

~ Grill the breasts skin-side up along with the cooked legs until golden and crispy, then flip over to finish the cooking on the underside.

PISTACHIO, MINT & ORANGE BLOSSOM SAUCE

~ Blend the first 4 ingredients together with 2 tablespoons water and 50g of the pistachios, then gradually blend in both the oils.

~ Toast (see page 106) and roughly chop the remaining pistachios.

~ Transfer the blended mixture to a bowl, then mix in the chopped nuts, herbs and salt. Check the seasoning and keep at room temperature.

PICKLED CARROTS

~ Bring the pickle liquor to the boil in a saucepan, add the orange blossom water and pour over the whole baby carrots in a bowl. Leave to cool to room temperature.

ASSEMBLE

~ Divide the quail breasts and legs between 4 warmed plates, alongside a wedge of lettuce, some radishes and pickled carrots, and a generous dollop of yogurt sprinkled with pepper.

~ Spoon a generous amount of the pistachio sauce over each plate.

SLOW-ROAST RACK OF ROSE VEAL, PARSLEY & SPENWOOD PISTOU

194

Rack of veal is a lovely cut, as well as quite significantly cheaper than fillet. In this recipe, by leaving the salt in contact with the meat for a prolonged time, the seasoning penetrates the veal in a way that seasoning with fine salt just before cooking would not achieve. The same applies to the fenugreek; it gives a delicious depth of flavour to the meat. Only season bigger cuts of meat this far in advance, and never tender cuts such as fillet, which would firm up in a way that would detract from their tenderness.

Roasting at a lower temperature will also give a more tender result than cooking the meat in a raging oven, as the protein firms up more gently, retaining its juices within rather than squeezing them out.

Pistou is basically pesto without the pine nuts, though this is a highly anglicised version using parsley and Spenwood cheese. Feel free to combine whatever cheeses and herbs take your fancy. Serve with simple roast potatoes.

VEAL

1kg veal rack on the bone

4 tablespoons coarse sea salt

4 tablespoons fenugreek seeds

extra virgin rapeseed oil

1 quantity Mayonnaise (see page 294), to serve

RUNNER BEANS

500g runner beans

garlic oil (shop-bought)

1 lemon

sea salt flakes

PISTOU

½ garlic clove

handful of baby spinach

50g parsley leaves

140g extra virgin olive oil

65g Spenwood cheese, finely grated

1 teaspoon caster sugar

pinch of fine sea salt

VEAL

- ~ Season the veal all over with the salt and fenugreek and leave for 2 hours, then wash off and pat the meat dry.
- ~ Preheat the oven to 130°C.
- ~ Colour the meat all over in a hot pan in the rapeseed oil, especially skin-side down to create a crackling.
- ~ Transfer to a roasting tray and cook for 45 minutes, or until the core temperature reaches 58°C.
- ~ Leave to rest somewhere warm for no less than 30 minutes.
- ~ Take the meat off the bone and carve it into 4 thick slices.

RUNNER BEANS

- ~ Blanch the runner beans in salted water for 1 minute, then refresh in iced water and store on kitchen paper.
- ~ Top and tail by cutting at an angle, then peel away the fibrous string that runs along both sides.
- ~ Toss in garlic oil and then grill in a hot chargrill pan on both sides, aggressively and quickly.
- ~ Place on a tray in a single layer, grate over lemon zest (ideally with a Microplane grater) and scatter with sea salt flakes.

PISTOU

- ~ Blend everything together in a blender to a coarse purée.

TO SERVE

- ~ Divide the runner beans between 4 warmed plates and spoon the pistou generously on top.
- ~ Place the veal alongside and serve with a dollop of mayonnaise.

GLAZED PORK RIBS WITH SAGE & CHILLI

I'm not a fan of Tex-Mex, nor barbecue sauce, nor indeed any preparations where you can't tell what is in them… but you know they aren't good for you. That means that pork ribs are not my choice of meal, as they usually come slathered in an unidentifiable sickly sweet brown sauce. This recipe is the perfect alternative. It offers the carnal pleasure, the sweet and sour, the tender meat, melting collagen and crispy fat, but with a clarity of flavour. What's more, it really couldn't be more simple and it works brilliantly.

Serve with jacket potatoes topped with good-quality cheese and a bitter leaf salad with artichoke hearts. It looks like there's a lot of ribs here, but remember that there is so much bone and that the meat shrinks during the long slow cooking. And three chillies may look like a lot, but this recipe can take them.

20g fine sea salt

90g white wine vinegar

120g soft brown sugar

300g olive oil

3 red chillies, deseeded and sliced

3 teaspoons dried oregano

leaves from 4 sage sprigs

6 garlic cloves, peeled

3 tablespoons clear honey

2kg pork ribs, separated individually

sea salt flakes, to serve (optional)

———

~ Preheat the oven to 150°C.

~ Blend all the ingredients, except the pork, together with 300g water, then mix with the ribs.

~ Place in a roasting tin in a nest of foil, and cover with more foil.

~ Cook in the oven for 2 hours, then open the foil and give it a stir. They won't look very promising at this point! Don't worry.

~ Increase the oven temperature to 180°C and return the ribs to the oven, this time without the foil covering, so the marinade can evaporate and reduce to a delicious glaze.

~ Divide between 4 warmed plates – or put on a big platter – and serve with finger bowls and plenty of napkins, with a bowl of salt flakes, if you like.

HAM HOCK WITH PARSLEY SAUCE

This is the sort of dish you start cooking at lunch time to be ready for dinner. The cooking time is long, but the preparation time very brief. It has all the comfort of a winter stew, but also a purity of flavour that elevates it beyond regular home cooking. The mustard seed tartare sauce adds a pleasing piquancy to cut through the sweet root vegetables and beans; it lifts the whole dish.

You can use good-quality canned white beans if that saves time, instead of soaking and cooking them from dried. Any left over ham hock is fantastic served alongside homemade Piccalilli (see page 295).

Serves 4–6

HAM

2 ham hocks, unsalted and unsmoked

8 rashers of smoked back bacon

2 garlic cloves, crushed

2 sage sprigs, bruised

VEGETABLES

200g dried white beans, soaked overnight in cold water, then drained

3 carrots, peeled and sliced 3cm thick on the angle

4 celery sticks, peeled of string and sliced 3cm thick on the angle

4 baby turnips, peeled and halved or quartered, depending on size

2 tablespoons shop-bought garlic oil, or olive oil

PARSLEY SAUCE

1 teaspoon fine sea salt

75g baby spinach

75g parsley leaves

TARTARE SAUCE

200g Mayonnaise (see page 294)

1 tablespoon wholegrain mustard

2 tablespoons rinsed and chopped gherkins

2 tablespoons rinsed and chopped capers

HAM

~ Place the ham hocks and 4 litres water into a pan that fits them snugly and ensures the meat is submerged.

~ Bring to a simmer, then cook over a low heat, or cover with foil and braise in an oven preheated to 130°C, for 5 hours. The meat is ready when the bones can be pulled out easily.

~ Add the bacon, garlic and sage to the pan, then leave to cool. The bacon will add a gentle smoky taste to the stock and season the meat.

~ Pass the liquor through a sieve and reserve. Flake the meat from the hocks into large neat pieces, discarding bone, gristle and thick fat. Keep the meat warm in some of the liquor.

VEGETABLES

~ Place the beans in a large saucepan and cover with 1 litre of the ham stock.

~ Simmer gently under a lid for 1 hour or until tender, then add the carrots, celery and turnips and cook until they are softened but still retain some texture. The turnips should be ready in 5 minutes, but the carrots could take up to 10. Remove each vegetable with a slotted spoon once it is ready.

~ Drain off the vegetables, reserving the liquor. Toss the vegetables with some garlic oil to glaze, then keep warm.

PARSLEY SAUCE

~ Bring 1 litre of the ham and vegetable cooking broth to the boil and add the salt and spinach. Blanch for 30 seconds, then add the parsley.

~ Blend straightaway to keep the raw parsley flavour and keep going for a full minute until the sauce is smooth and a vibrant green colour.

TARTARE SAUCE

~ Mix all the ingredients together.

TO SERVE

~ Mix the warm flaked ham hock, beans and vegetables together, then divide among 4–6 warmed bowls.

~ Pour over the parsley sauce and serve with the mustard seed tartare sauce.

CHARGRILLED IBERICO PORK, CELERIAC SALAD & OREGANO DRESSING

Iberico pork comes from the same animals that are reared for jamón and is red meat, so should be cooked medium rare. Presa is a large tender cut from between the neck and the shoulder of these special beasts.

DRESSING

1 teaspoon fine sea salt

½ teaspoon cornflour, dissolved in 2 tablespoons water

1 tablespoon dried oregano

pinch of chilli flakes

1 garlic clove, crushed

75g olive oil

50g Cabernet Sauvignon vinegar

25g parsley leaves and stems, chopped

IBERICO PORK

800g Iberico pork *presa*

2 tablespoons fenugreek seeds

garlic oil (shop-bought)

CELERIAC

1 celeriac, peeled and shredded

1 teaspoon fine sea salt

finely grated zest and juice of 1 lemon

2 tablespoons Chardonnay vinegar

4 tablespoons Mayonnaise (page 294)

3 tablespoons Greek yogurt

1 teaspoon Dijon mustard

1 teaspoon wholegrain mustard

DRESSING

~ Bring 100g water and the salt to the boil. Whisk in the cornflour solution, then return to the boil to thicken. Add the dried oregano and chilli flakes, then leave to cool.

~ Blend in the garlic and oil, the vinegar and parsley and leave overnight.

IBERICO PORK

~ Season the pork with the fenugreek seeds and leave for at least 2 hours, though preferably overnight.

~ Wash off and pat the meat dry. Season well all over and rub with garlic oil. Preheat the oven to 130°C.

~ Colour in a hot chargrill pan on all sides until smoky and deep golden.

~ Transfer to a roasting tray and cook for 15 minutes, until the core temperature reaches 56°C.

~ Rest on a warmed plate under foil for 15 minutes, then carve into 4 pieces.

CELERIAC

~ Mix the celeriac, salt, lemon zest and juice and vinegar, then cover and leave for 2 hours. Mix in the mayonnaise, yogurt and both types of mustard.

TO SERVE

~ Divide the celeriac between plates, add the pork and spoon over the dressing.

COTTAGE PIE
WITH RED WINE
& SMOKED BACON

206

This dish successfully combines all the comfort and nostalgia of shepherd's pie but with the smoky savouriness and yielding texture of a beef bourgignon. Featherblade is an underused cut of meat that is very reasonably priced and good for stewing: gelatinous but not as much so as shin.

Crisping the exterior of the mash in this recipe is important, because it gives a satisfying crust and contrasting texture to the softness of what lies beneath. You could even sprinkle it with some grated salty cheese, to accentuate the crunch. Running a fork through the mash increases its surface area, so there is more of it to crisp up, in much the same way as fluffing up boiled potatoes before roasting them. Serve with lightly cooked buttered Hispi cabbage.

Serves 6–8

FILLING

800g beef featherblade, cut into large chunks

2 tablespoons plain flour

2 tablespoons vegetable oil

2 tablespoons salted butter

2 onions, peeled and cut into segments

3 carrots, peeled and chopped into 1cm rounds

3 celery sticks, peeled of string and sliced across into 3cm pieces

300g pancetta, rind removed, cut into fat lardons

150g chestnut mushrooms, quartered

375g red wine

600g beef stock

2 garlic cloves, crushed

leaves from 4 thyme sprigs, chopped

6 turns of black pepper

1 teaspoon cornflour (optional)

fine sea salt

MASH

1.5kg Desiree potatoes

150g whole milk

150g unsalted butter

ASSEMBLE

10cm bone marrow (optional)

FILLING

- ~ Preheat the oven to 150°C.
- ~ Season the beef well with fine salt then dust in the flour, shaking off excess.
- ~ Heat a large heavy-based pan until very hot, then add the vegetable oil.
- ~ Colour the beef in batches until golden brown all over, adding the butter at the end to help with the caramelisation of the meat.
- ~ Once browned, remove the meat using tongs and place on a plate, but keep the pan over the heat and add the onions, carrots, celery, pancetta and mushrooms.
- ~ Season very lightly (as the pancetta is salty) and cook until light golden.
- ~ Return the beef to the pan. Now pour in the wine and bring to the boil for 1 minute to remove some of its acidity and alcohol. Add the stock and return to a simmer.
- ~ Cover with a lid and place in the oven. Braise for 2 hours until tender.
- ~ Add the garlic, thyme and black pepper, and mix through. I add these aromats at the end so you can taste the pungency of garlic, and the thyme retains its freshness of flavour. Check the seasoning. If the gravy needs to be thickened slightly, add the cornflour dissolved in a little water, then return to the boil to thicken.

MASH

- ~ Peel the potatoes and cut into quarters if large or halves if small. They should be large pieces so they can't absorb too much water. They must also be evenly sized, so they cook at the same rate.
- ~ Place the potatoes, 5 litres water and 3 tablespoons salt in a large saucepan, bring to a simmer and cook very gently, just bubbling, for about 30 minutes, or until cooked through completely but not falling apart.
- ~ Drain well through a colander and leave for 5 minutes to allow the steam to escape, then transfer the potatoes to a bowl and mash well, adding the milk, butter and 2 teaspoons salt to create a smooth, fluffy mix.

ASSEMBLE

- ~ Preheat the oven to 200°C. If you are using the bone marrow, place it upright in the centre of an oven dish, surrounded by the beef filling. Or just spoon in the filling, if not using the marrow.
- ~ Top the beef with the mash, then run a fork through it to create waves.
- ~ Cook for 15 minutes, until golden on top, then, if needed, glaze under a hot grill to crisp the top further.
- ~ Serve in the oven dish for everyone to help themselves.

ROAST PORK BELLY, WHITE BEANS, SWEETCORN & LOVAGE

This method of cooking pork belly is rooted in Chinese cuisine. It produces delicious results with little fuss, though you do need to start the process a couple of days beforehand. In this recipe it is served with a simple but very moreish salad. The sweetcorn, starchy beans, grassy lovage and acidic vinegar combine to create something both satisfying and complex.

PORK

1kg pork belly, on the bone, skin scored

100g white wine vinegar

4 tablespoons fenugeek seeds

2 handfuls of coarse salt

SWEETCORN SALAD

200g sweetcorn kernels, drained

200g butter beans, drained and rinsed

100g cherry tomatoes, halved

2 tablespoons white balsamic or Chardonnay vinegar

4 tablespoons Lemon dressing (see page 294)

½ garlic clove, finely grated

4 spring onions, sliced on the angle

4 tablespoons chopped lovage or parsley leaves

1 small green chilli, halved, deseeded and finely sliced on the angle

pinch of fine sea salt

PORK

- Place the pork in a pan of water and boil for 10 minutes. Drain. Pat dry.

- Place the vinegar in a tray then top with the pork, skin-side down. This helps create lighter, puffier crackling.

- Sprinkle the fenugreek on the flesh, then top with a tray and heavy weight. Leave overnight. Rinse, then pat dry and air-dry overnight, skin-side up.

- Next day, preheat the oven to 170°C.

- Crimp foil around the belly to cover all sides tightly and come up 1cm from the top. Skewer under the skin with 2 metal skewers corner to corner, then top with the salt. (It looks a lot, but it gets scraped off.) Cook for 1 hour.

- Remove the pork from the oven and increase the temperature to 220°C.

- Remove the skewers and foil and brush away all the salt. Return to the oven for 20 minutes to crisp the skin.

- Rest for a minimum of 30 minutes.

SWEETCORN SALAD

- Mix everything together and check the seasoning. It should be quite sharp.

TO SERVE

- Remove the rib bones and carve the pork into finger-width slices.

- Serve the salad with the pork belly.

SPICED LAMB MEATBALLS WITH CHICKPEAS & FETA

Good meatballs are one of the most satisfying things to eat, and the secret is in their softness. Rather than being a tight ball of meat, they should be soft and indulgent. This is achieved through a panade: a mix of egg, bread and milk that effectively dilutes the protein content for a more yielding, comforting result. There is a distinct nod to Greece here, though there is nothing authentic about this dish. This is the recipe I cook the most for myself at home. The cinnamon adds a lovely warmth to the sauce and the salad a freshness. You can use a mix of minced beef and pork, if you prefer it to lamb.

Serves 6

MEATBALL MIX

4 slices of white bread, without crust, torn

100g whole milk

1 egg, lightly beaten

800g minced lamb

1 garlic clove, finely grated

½ teaspoon Dijon mustard

½ teaspoon dried oregano

1 teaspoon onion powder

1 teaspoon fine sea salt

½ teaspoon crushed black pepper

1 teaspoon fennel seeds, crushed

¼ teaspoon cayenne pepper

¼ teaspoon ground mace

plain flour, to dust

SAUCE

100g olive oil

1 small aubergine, chopped into 4–5cm pieces

1 large red onion, core removed, cut into segments

2 garlic cloves, crushed

400g can of chopped tomatoes

½ cinnamon stick

1 tablespoon Chardonnay vinegar

2 teaspoons caster sugar

1 teaspoon fine sea salt

400g can of chickpeas, drained and rinsed

1 small courgette, halved and sliced on the angle into 3cm pieces

ASSEMBLE

150g feta cheese, crumbled

16 cherry vine tomatoes, halved

¼ bunch mint leaves, roughly chopped

¼ bunch parsley leaves, roughly chopped

¼ cucumber, peeled, halved and sliced finely on the angle

2 handfuls of rocket

juice of ½ lemon

MEATBALL MIX

~ Combine the bread, milk and egg together well in a large bowl to form a paste. Leave to soak and hydrate for 30 minutes.

~ Add the remaining ingredients except the flour and mix thoroughly.

~ Sprinkle some flour on to a tray and have a bowl of it to dust your hands.

~ Roll the meat mixture into large balls, each about 60g, and place on the floured tray, dusting with more flour on top.

SAUCE

~ Preheat the oven to 160°C.

~ Heat a wide casserole and add some of the olive oil. Add the meatballs and fry until golden brown all over.

~ Remove the meatballs with a slotted spoon and place on a plate.

~ In the same pan, add the remaining oil, aubergine and onion and fry until light golden, then add the garlic and cook for a minute. Season with salt.

~ Add the tomatoes, then pour in 400g water and add the cinnamon stick, vinegar, sugar and salt and mix well. Return to a simmer and cook for 5 minutes, then mix in the chickpeas.

~ Return the meatballs to the pan and toss them in the sauce. Cover with a lid and place in the oven.

~ Bake for 30 minutes, then add the courgette and cook for another 10 minutes. Remove from the oven, take off the lid and allow to cool for 5 minutes.

ASSEMBLE

~ Mix together all the salad ingredients in a bowl and scatter over the meatballs in the casserole, then take the pan to the table.

GRILLED LAMB CUTLETS, VIOLET MUSTARD, CRUSHED GREEN HERBS

Violet mustard is a product you will need to buy online, but it keeps very well in the refrigerator. It is sweet and spicy and very addictive, so it's definitely worth having a pot in your kitchen.

The crushed green herbs here are, for me, a staple, and also keep very well once chilled. These go with just about anything, from grilled meats and fish to flatbreads and roasted vegetables, so do make extra for another meal.

CRUSHED GREEN HERBS

200g olive oil

1 garlic clove, sliced

½ teaspoon smoked paprika

50g parsley leaves and stems

25g coriander leaves and stems

100g green pepper, finely chopped

25g banana shallot, finely chopped

3 tablespoons red wine vinegar
(Cabernet Sauvignon if possible)

1 tablespoon cumin seeds, toasted
(see page 19)

fine sea salt

LAMB

16 lamb chops or cutlets

2 tablespoons olive oil

violet mustard

CRUSHED GREEN HERBS

217

~ Blend the oil, garlic, smoked paprika and a pinch of salt with 50g water until the sliced garlic has disappeared.

~ Add the herbs and blend to a coarse green mix.

~ Remove from the blender, transfer to a bowl and mix in the green pepper, shallot, vinegar and cumin.

LAMB

~ Preheat the grill to its highest setting.

~ Season the lamb chops well all over, then roll in the olive oil.

~ Grill the lamb under a fierce heat for 1–2 minutes on each side, depending on the heat of the grill and the thickness of the meat, turning as needed, until well coloured but still pink within. Alternatively, cook on a barbecue or in a chargrill pan.

~ Leave the meat to rest under some loose foil for 5 minutes.

TO SERVE

~ Brush each chop with violet mustard, then serve immediately with a bowl of the crushed green herbs.

VENISON TOAD-IN-THE-HOLE & ONION GRAVY

Any sausages could be used here, they don't have to be venison. The batter is a rare recipe that uses volume rather than weight as a measure; use a small- to medium-sized tea or coffee cup. Alternatively, start with 4 eggs and use an equal volume of flour and milk.

The gravy recipe here is intended to be a simple homely one that would be perfect with this dish or a Sunday roast. (If the latter, then omit the caramelised onions.) Use it as a blueprint and change the meat used accordingly, depending on what you are serving it with. This kind of gravy can be unavoidably expensive to make, as you do need some stewing meat or bones as the main ingredient, but you can eat that meat and the vegetables, too: I mix in a little cream and use them as a sauce for gnocchi. Serve this with some buttered cabbage and roast carrots.

BATTER

1 cup plain flour

1 teaspoon fine sea salt

1 cup whole eggs

1 cup semi-skimmed milk

SAUSAGES

8 venison sausages

50g vegetable oil

CARAMELISED ONIONS

2 large white onions, halved, then finely sliced

2 tablespoons vegetable oil

1 teaspoon caster sugar

1 tablespoon sherry vinegar

fine sea salt

GRAVY

1kg stewing beef, chopped

1 Spanish onion, quartered

2 field mushrooms, halved

1 carrot, halved

1 celery stick, halved

1 beefsteak tomato, halved

1 teaspoon fine sea salt

200ml red wine

200ml white wine

2 tablespoons cornflour

2 thyme sprigs, bruised

1 rosemary sprig, bruised

1 garlic clove, crushed

1 teaspoon sherry vinegar

BATTER

~ Put the flour and salt into a bowl. Place the eggs and milk in a jug and whisk together, then whisk into the flour just until combined.

~ Leave to rest in the refrigerator for a couple of hours.

SAUSAGES

~ Preheat the oven to 160°C.

~ Place the sausages in an ovenproof dish lined with baking parchment and cook for 15 minutes.

~ Remove the paper and pour in the oil, return the dish to the oven and increase the temperature to 240°C.

~ Heat for 3 minutes, then pour in the batter and immediately shut the oven door.

~ Reduce the oven temperature to 220°C and cook for 25 minutes, until golden brown and cooked through.

CARAMELISED ONIONS

~ Caramelise the onions in a hot pan in the vegetable oil with a pinch of salt and the sugar until brown and sweetened, about 30 minutes (be patient), then add the vinegar and remove from the heat.

GRAVY

~ Preheat the oven to 220°C.

~ Spread the meat and vegetables out in a roasting tray and season with the 1 teaspoon salt. Roast until golden brown all over, about 30 minutes

~ Transfer to a large stockpot, including any fat and juices from the tray.

~ Meanwhile, bring both the wines to the boil in a separate saucepan, then remove from the heat.

~ Add the wine to the stockpot with 1.5 litres water, then place over a low heat and simmer gently for 90 minutes.

~ Strain well through a colander, then return to the heat.

~ In a small bowl, whisk the cornflour with 4 tablespoons water, then add to the gravy. Bring to the boil to thicken, then add the remaining ingredients and leave to infuse for 5 minutes.

~ Pass the gravy through a sieve, squeezing well on the aromats, then add the caramelised onions.

TO SERVE

~ Serve the toad-in-the-hole in the middle of the table with a jug of gravy for people to help themselves.

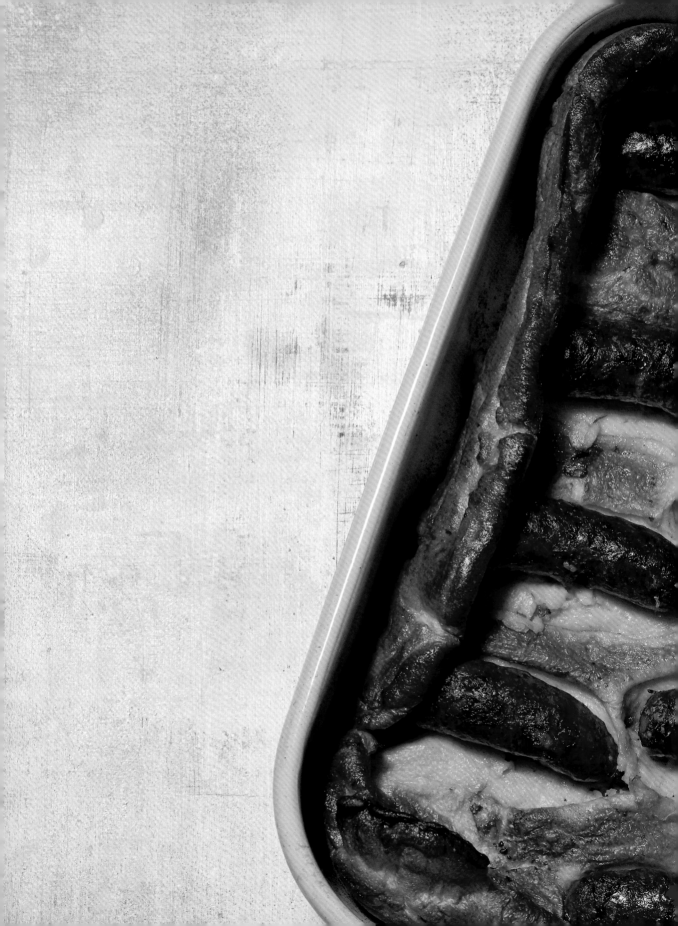

ROAST VENISON WITH JERUSALEM ARTICHOKES, TARRAGON & RYE

Game can conjure fear in some people, but this recipe is a very gentle introduction, an easy to make, delicious winter dish that is beautifully balanced. Feel free to substitute the tarragon emulsion for some mayonnaise mixed with a healthy amount of chopped tarragon and a splash of Chardonnay vinegar, if you want to save time.

Venison haunch is often available from butchers, but is made up of different muscles, some of which are better than others. If this is your first time cooking with venison, I recommend you start with the loin, which is always tender throughout. The Jerusalem artichoke broth is delicious in its own right.

ARTICHOKE BROTH

500g Jerusalem artichokes, peeled, halved and sliced 1cm thick (no less)

4 tablespoons extra virgin olive oil

2 teaspoons fine sea salt

2 teaspoons caster sugar

juice of ½ lemon

1 litre whole milk

2 tablespoons Chardonnay vinegar

1 teaspoon truffle oil

RYE BREADCRUMBS

4 slices of rye or pumpernickel bread

TARRAGON EMULSION

20g tarragon

2 egg yolks

2 tablespoons Chardonnay vinegar

100g vegetable oil

35g extra virgin olive oil

fine sea salt

PICKLED ARTICHOKES

250g pickle liquor (see page 304)

4 large Jerusalem artichokes, scrubbed

VENISON

4 x 150g venison loins, trimmed

vegetable oil

salted butter

leaves from 4 thyme sprigs

1 teaspoon juniper seeds, crushed to a powder

ASSEMBLE

1 tablespoon caraway seeds, lightly toasted (see page 19)

4 pinches of tarragon leaves

ARTICHOKE BROTH

~ In a deep, covered sauté pan, sweat the Jerusalem artichokes in the olive oil with the salt, sugar and lemon juice for 10 minutes, until softened and cooking in their own juice.

~ Bring the milk separately to the boil, then pour it on to the artichokes.

~ Simmer over a medium-high heat for 10 minutes, or until the artichokes are just cooked, to keep their crisp, fresh flavour; don't overcook them.

~ Remove from the heat and blend with the vinegar and truffle oil in a good blender until completely smooth; it should be light, not thick. Pass through a sieve.

RYE BREADCRUMBS

~ Cut the bread into pieces, then blitz in a blender to coarse crumbs.

TARRAGON EMULSION

~ Blend the tarragon, egg yolks, vinegar and a pinch of salt together with 2 tablespoons water, then gradually add both the oils to emulsify.

~ Keep in the refrigerator until needed.

PICKLED ARTICHOKES

~ Bring the pickle liquor to the boil.

~ Slice the artichokes across into thin slices (about 2mm) using a mandolin, then place in a bowl and pour over the pickle liquor. Cover and leave to cool to room temperature

VENISON

~ Preheat the oven to 130°C.

~ Season the venison all over with salt.

~ Colour quickly on all sides in a hot pan in some vegetable oil, then add a little butter to encourage the browning process for another minute.

~ Transfer to a roasting tray and cook for about 5 minutes, until the core temperature is 52°C.

~ Leave to rest for 15 minutes, then rub with the thyme and season lightly with the juniper. Carve into 1.5cm slices.

ASSEMBLE

~ Spoon 2 tablespoons of rye crumbs and 1 tablespoon of tarragon emulsion into 4 warmed bowls, then top with the sliced venison.

~ Top with the pickled artichoke shavings in a neat layer, then finally a sprinkling of caraway seeds and a scattering of tarragon leaves.

~ Serve with a jug of the hot Jerusalem artichoke broth.

CHICKEN PIE

This recipe is a meal in itself, but can obviously be served alongside some mashed potato and gravy, if you like. The decoration on top is optional, but it is far easier than you think. Just scatter it on and you can't go wrong.

Serves 6–8

BECHAMEL

500g whole milk

½ white onion, peeled and sliced

2 cloves

¼ teaspoon ground mace

pinch of cayenne pepper

1 teaspoon Dijon mustard

1 teaspoon fine sea salt

50g unsalted butter

25g plain flour

PIE FILLING

8 corn-fed chicken thighs

4 tablespoons garlic oil (shop-bought)

2 carrots, peeled and quartered, then sliced across into 1cm pieces

25g salted butter

1 leek, quartered, then sliced across into 1cm pieces

1 celery stick, peeled of string, halved, then sliced across into 1cm pieces

100g shiitake mushrooms, halved

3 garlic cloves, crushed

200g canned sweetcorn, drained

100g frozen peas, defrosted

2 tablespoons chopped thyme leaves

2 tablespoons chopped tarragon leaves

finely grated zest of ½ lemon

ASSEMBLE

1 egg yolk

2 tablespoons milk or cream (any type)

2 sheets of frozen puff pastry, defrosted

TO DECORATE (OPTIONAL)

spring onions, shredded

red onions, cut into slim petals

fennel fronds

tarragon sprigs

pansies

————

BECHAMEL

~ Bring the milk to the boil in a saucepan then add the onion, spices, mustard and salt. Cover and leave to infuse for 20 minutes. Pass through a sieve.

~ Heat the butter in a large saucepan, stir in the flour and mix until smooth.

~ Add the hot infused milk a bit at a time and whisk to combine until smooth. Once all the milk has been added, bring to the boil, whisking continuously, then remove from the heat.

PIE FILLING

~ Preheat the oven to 180°C.

~ Season the chicken with salt and roll it in the garlic oil, then place on a roasting tray and cook for 40 minutes, skin-side up, until the skin is crispy and the meat is tender.

~ Leave to rest for 20 minutes. Discard the bone and sinew and flake the meat, reserving any juices. You don't need the skin here, but you can use it for an extra decoration of chicken crackling, if you like. (Or just eat it.)

~ Sweat the carrots in the butter in a sauté pan for 5 minutes, lid on, then add the leek and celery. Season lightly with salt, cover and cook for another 5 minutes. Add the mushrooms and garlic, cover and cook for a final 5 minutes.

~ Add the sweetcorn, peas, thyme and tarragon, then remove from the heat and mix in the chicken and bechamel with the lemon zest. Check the seasoning and leave to cool.

ASSEMBLE

~ Preheat the oven to 190°C.

~ Mix the egg yolk and milk or cream in a small bowl to make an egg wash.

~ From the first sheet of pastry, cut out a circle using the top of an ovenproof frying pan as a guide. This is the lid.

~ Cut a circle of greaseproof paper large enough to cover the base of the same ovenproof frying pan and come all the way up the sides. Use this as a guide to cut out a circle of pastry of the same size. This is the base. Place the circle of pastry in the pan, pushing it flat against the sides.

~ Fill with the cooled chicken pie mix, making sure it doesn't cover the top of the pastry rim.

~ Top with the pastry lid, pinching the edges of both pastry circles together to crimp and join.

~ With some of the pastry trim, you may cut out some leaf shapes or make a simple lattice to garnish the pie.

~ Brush with egg wash and leave for 10 minutes, then brush again with egg wash and place in the oven.

~ Cook for 20 minutes, then reduce the oven temperature to 170°C and cook for another 20 minutes.

TO DECORATE

~ Scatter over the vegetables, herbs and flowers, if using, and return the pie to the oven for a final 5 minutes for the decorations to crisp up, then serve.

MINCE & DUMPLINGS

My version of the traditional school food, but with a few changes. In this recipe, the swede adds a lovely heartiness to the dish, while the tomato ketchup and mustard respectively lend sweetness and heat.

The biggest bastardisation from the original is the addition of milk and yeast to the dumplings, which does lighten them to give them a texture, delicacy and colour not dissimilar to an Asian steamed bun.

The parsley should only be roughly chopped, not finely, so it keeps that grassy edge to offset the rich flavours of the mince.

DUMPLINGS

125g tepid whole milk

5g fast-action dried yeast

180g strong white bread flour

5g fine sea salt

5g caster sugar

95g shredded suet

MINCE

2 tablespoons vegetable oil

800g minced beef

2 teaspoons fine sea salt

1 white onion, peeled and finely chopped

½ swede, peeled and finely chopped

1 carrot, peeled and finely chopped

1 celery stick, finely chopped

1 tablespoon plain flour

100g red wine

100g white wine

50g tomato ketchup

10g Dijon mustard

15g Worcestershire sauce

750g beef stock

a few turns of black pepper

1 garlic clove, crushed

1 bay leaf

leaves from 2 thyme sprigs, finely chopped

needles from 2 rosemary sprigs, finely chopped

ASSEMBLE

parsley leaves, roughly chopped

DUMPLINGS

~ Mix together the milk and yeast to dissolve, then place in the bowl of a food mixer fitted with a dough hook.

~ Add the dry ingredients and knead for 5 minutes until smooth.

~ Place the ball of dough in a bowl and leave to prove, covered, for 1 hour at room temperature.

~ Divide into 50g pieces, then roll each piece into a ball.

~ Place on a baking tray lined with greaseproof paper, allowing 5cm gaps between each dumpling.

~ Cover the dumplings with a damp new J-cloth and leave to prove once more for 2 hours until well risen.

MINCE

~ Heat a large saucepan over a high heat until very hot, then add the oil, then the minced meat.

~ Add 1 teaspoon of the salt and fry until well browned all over, breaking up any lumps with a wooden spoon.

~ Season the vegetables with another 1 teaspoon salt and mix, then add to the pan and cook for 5 minutes.

~ Add the flour and stir to coat.

~ Add both the wines and bring to the boil, scraping the base of the pan.

~ Add the ketchup, mustard, Worcestershire sauce, stock, black pepper, garlic and herbs. Stir well to combine.

~ Transfer to a flameproof casserole and top the beef evenly with the dumplings, then cover with a lid and simmer for 1 hour over a gentle heat.

ASSEMBLE

~ Scatter generously with chopped parsley and serve.

FRUIT &
BERRIES

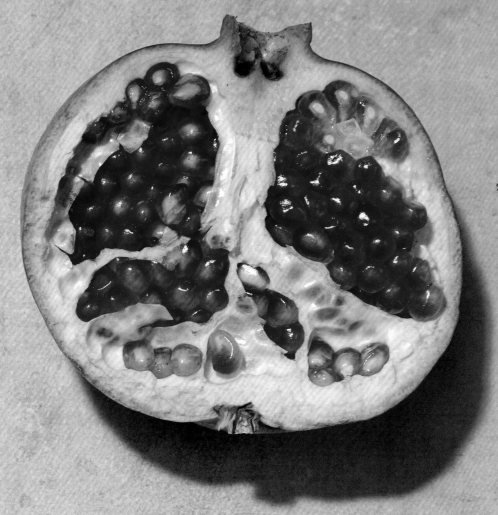

235

236

Ripe fruit at its best – natural and unadorned – is truly memorable, better than any constructed dessert could be. However, it is often not accessible in cooler climates. If I lived in Italy or the south of France, rather than in the UK, I would be perfectly happy to finish every meal with a ripe peach or a handful of flawless figs. As I don't, something more elaborate is called for.

All my favourite desserts are based on fruit and I like to display the fragrance and flavour of truly great fruit through simplicity and restraint, so that it retains as much of its integrity as possible. Other flavours are there merely to complement the fruit, not to mask it. Often, I will add a lactic or buttery counterpoint, which, rather than diluting the natural taste of the fruit, will highlight it, providing a rich base through which the fruit can burst, as dairy fat prolongs on the palate all the flavours with which it is paired.

It comes naturally to me to mix fruits – especially summer fruits – with aromatic herbs, such as rose, lemon verbena, basil, lavender or fig leaf. I think of them as seasonings to supplement fruit's lush, ripe qualities. A ripe peach, for example, is incredibly juicy, succulent and fragrant and I'd rather flatter it with lavender than pour melted chocolate over it, blend it with cream or chop the juicy flesh into oblivion. For me, that would be to obscure the perfect fruit.

When I first started work at Le Manoir aux Quat' Saisons 20 years ago, almost all the best fruit in the UK was imported from France or Italy. French strawberries, for instance, were better than British. These days, British farmers have really upped their game and, as a country, our self-sufficiency in high-quality fruit has soared.

This is excellent news for us cooks, who don't always have the time to bake a cake, or to infuse a syrup with flowers. If you run out of time, simply serve very good fruit naked, 'seasoned' with a light sprinkling of sugar and a squeeze of lemon juice, then add a scattering of mint or basil leaves to transform it into something elegant, fragrant and delicious. (Fruit contains a great deal of fructose already, so use a light hand with the sugar.) Feel free to pour over a splash of Prosecco or some iced tea, too.

Most importantly, remember to allow time for your fruit to ripen, so you may need to buy it a couple of days before you intend to use it.

Raspberries are at their best in late summer. In this chapter, they are marbled with a gentle cloud-like vanilla rice pudding to create a ripple effect. I've given two strawberry desserts: one using wild strawberries in a tartlet with a rich camomile custard and rose petals steeped in syrup: a strawberry tart is always a crowd-pleaser in the summer, and for good reason. I also make regular strawberries into a charlotte: a fancy French affair that looks fantastic, a bit like glorified strawberries and cream, with some soaked trifle sponges and basil leaves. The lemon verbena posset is incredibly simple to make; it has the ideal balance of sweet and sour and the verbena adds a lovely sherbet-like edge. The cooking process is a perfect alchemy whereby the acidity of the lemon 'cooks' the cream, causing it to set once chilled.

Yorkshire rhubarb is celebrated in a crumble, but no ordinary one. The crumble recipe here is slightly different to the conventional version. By cooking it separately from the fruit, you get a crunchier and crumblier result; the mix is less condensed. Also, adding plenty of porridge oats makes the crumble lighter and more digestible without losing any of that traditional crumble satisfaction. It's also versatile: if not rhubarb and rose water, traditional apple and blackberry will always raise a smile, or even try pear and raspberry if you fancy a change.

Various different fruits could be added to the clafoutis recipe, too, depending on what is in season, though whatever you add it will be delicious. Somewhere between a sponge cake and a custard, when clafoutis comes out of the oven and is still warm – but not hot – it is hard to think of another pudding you would swap it for.

Cakes always seem more fitting at home than in a restaurant. The fig leaf cake in this chapter is very striking; the batter is baked in a parcel formed by the leaves. As they bake, they release their subtle flavour that imbues the cake. It is absolutely delicious, and well worth finding some fig trees for!

The sweet potato I use in a cake in this chapter sounds a bit wrong, but it has a classic carrot cake as a blueprint. It is an autumnal affair. The sweet potato ensures the cake is beautifully moist, while argan oil adds a complementary nuttiness. Don't be afraid to use vegetables in cakes; fennel, for instance, is amazing grated into a plain sponge cake batter with grated apple and Earl Grey tea (don't worry about the texture of the grated vegetable; the fennel just dissolves into the mixture during the baking process).

The garden cupcake is perhaps the most finessed cake recipe here and, don't worry, its frosting is far from the sickly sweet topping of regular cupcakes. However, for maximum retro effect, do seek out a star-shaped nozzle when piping your refined frosting on…

RHUBARB, ROSE WATER & POPPY SEED CRUMBLE

238

Forced rhubarb is a British ingredient worthy of celebrating. Grown in the charmingly named 'rhubarb triangle' between Rothwell, Morley and Wakefield in West Yorkshire, it is very much a labour of love. After the first frosts, rhubarb is transplanted into dark sheds and gentle heat is applied, creating accelerated growth. It is harvested by hand in candlelight, and the stalks are a vivid red, far sweeter and more tender than the regular outdoor variety.

Cooking the rhubarb and crumble separately first gives a more polished end result than baking the raw crumble mix over the fruit.

RHUBARB COMPOTE

500g forced rhubarb, plus 175g, all cut into 2cm pieces

100g caster sugar, plus 30g

juice of ½ lemon

1 tablespoon rose water

CRUMBLE

75g salted butter, chopped

75g plain flour

75g soft brown sugar

75g jumbo porridge oats

10g poppy seeds (optional)

ASSEMBLE

clotted cream

lavender flowers, or other edible flowers

RHUBARB COMPOTE

~ Cook the 500g rhubarb with the 100g sugar and the lemon juice in a saucepan set over a medium heat for 10 minutes, stirring until it is cooked, but hasn't produced too much liquid. Keep the lid on for the first couple of minutes to produce steam, then remove it to evaporate the liquid.

~ Strain through a colander over a bowl, to remove the excess liquid. After straining, it should weigh 400g.

~ Mix the remaining 175g rhubarb and 30g sugar together and then mix into the compote with the rose water.

CRUMBLE

~ Preheat the oven to 160°C.

~ Mix everything together in a food mixer until it resembles coarse crumbs, then transfer to a baking tray.

~ Bake for 25 minutes, stirring every 10 minutes, until golden and crunchy. Leave to cool.

ASSEMBLE

~ Preheat the oven to 180°C.

~ Spread the rhubarb in a gratin dish and sprinkle over the crumble.

~ Cook for 20 minutes, then leave to cool for 5 minutes.

~ Serve with the clotted cream scattered with lavender, or other edible flowers.

FIG LEAF CAKE

This cake tastes like a holiday somewhere warm. The fig leaves give it a delicious flavour as it cooks, not dissimilar to coconut, hence the use of that oil in this recipe. Though quite exotic in character, the cake couldn't be simpler to make.

The fragrance as it comes out the oven is amazing, so make sure all your windows are closed, to get the full benefit! Fig leaves are great in any dairy-based dessert, such as custards, ice creams or panna cottas.

If they are very fresh, the leaves will be quite stiff and harder to use, but if you freeze and defrost them, they become more malleable.

Serves 8–10

unsalted butter, for the tin

280g golden caster sugar

240g plain flour

100g ground almonds

200g whole milk

150g coconut oil

2 large eggs

1 vanilla pod, split lengthways, seeds scraped out

1 teaspoon baking powder

1 teaspoon bicarbonate of soda

pinch of fine sea salt

4 fig leaves, plus 6 (optional) for the 'crown'

6 figs, halved

2 tablespoons clear honey, melted

~ Preheat the oven to 170°C. Butter and fully line a 26cm springform cake tin.

~ Place the first 10 ingredients in a mixing bowl, and beat until smooth. Gradually whisk in 75g boiling water. The mix will be quite wet.

~ Place 4 fig leaves over the base and sides of the tin. Place the fig halves on the base, spaced apart, cut-sides down.

~ Pour in the batter, ensuring it goes between the figs. Bake for 50 minutes, until cooked but still moist within: a skewer will come out clean. Leave to cool for 10 minutes, then turn out.

~ If you wish to make the crown, arrange the 6 fig leaves on a baking tray so they all point outwards in a large circle. Sit the baked cake on top, then fold the leaves up the sides and over the top of the cake. They should stick to it.

~ Place the opened springform cake tin over this. Unfold the leaves so they don't rest on the cake. Fill the space on top with crumpled baking parchment, to stop the leaves falling inwards.

~ Return to the oven at 170°C for 10–15 minutes until the leaves are dry and stand upright. Surprisingly, this won't overbake the cake as it is almost pudding-like and very forgiving. Remove the tin and carefully transfer the cake to a serving plate.

~ Serve just warm, the top brushed lightly with the melted honey.

WILD STRAWBERRY & ROSE PETAL TARTLET

242

The candied rose petals here are a revelation, lifting the tartlets into something fragrant, quirky and esoteric. The lavender also pairs well with the floral notes in wild strawberries, though if those are not available, just use ripe regular strawberries, sliced. The custard and the pastry provide a fat and carbohydrate content substantial enough to prevent the floral flavours from dominating. The rose petals are best made a day before so they can infuse in the syrup; this also spreads the work load. You'll need 4 x 10cm tartlet tins or rings.

SWEET PASTRY

125g salted butter, softened

75g icing sugar

30g ground almonds

finely grated zest of ½ lemon

1 small egg, lightly beaten

225g plain flour

1 egg yolk

2 tablespoons whipping cream

ROSE PETALS

50g rose water

100g caster sugar

juice of ½ lemon

a drop of red food colouring, or some beetroot colour

1 unsprayed red rose, petals separated

PASTRY CREAM

500g whole milk

2 camomile teabags

½ vanilla pod, split lengthways, seeds scraped out (optional)

6 egg yolks

75g caster sugar

1 tablespoon clear honey

40g cornflour

300g double cream, whipped to firm peaks

ASSEMBLE

4 tablespoons strawberry purée (optional)

8 tablespoons wild strawberries

1 tablespoon lavender flowers

1 tablespoon icing sugar

———

SWEET PASTRY

~ Mix together the butter, icing sugar, almonds and zest in a food mixer fitted with the paddle attachment.

~ Once everything has been combined, beat in the egg, followed by the flour.

~ Flatten out into a 4cm-thick disc, wrap in cling film and chill for at least 12 hours before use.

~ Take the dough out of the refrigerator for 10 minutes, to allow it to soften.

~ Roll it to 1.5mm thick between sheets of baking parchment, then return to the refrigerator and chill for 1 hour.

~ Preheat the oven to 160°C.

~ Cut out rings of pastry big enough to line 4 x 10cm tart cases or rings, then carefully line them, pushing down in the edges to get a neat outline.

~ Mix the egg yolk and whipping cream in a small bowl to make the egg wash.

~ Place the cases on a baking tray and bake for 15–20 minutes until golden.

~ Remove the cases or rings, then brush the inside of the tartlet shells with the egg wash and return to the oven for 2–3 minutes, to seal the pastry. Cool on a wire rack.

~ Use a vegetable peeler or a Microplane to neaten the pastry edges.

ROSE PETALS

~ Heat all the ingredients, except the petals, in a pan with 100g water.

~ Bring 4 litres of water to a simmer and add the petals. Blanch until softened and speckled, about 3 minutes.

~ Using a slotted spoon, transfer the petals to the rose water syrup.

~ Leave to cool to room temperature, then let them soak in the syrup for at least 4 hours, or preferably overnight.

~ When needed, remove from the syrup and open out on to a plate.

PASTRY CREAM

~ Bring the milk to the boil, remove from the heat and add the teabags and vanilla, if using. Cover with cling film, leave to infuse for 30 minutes, then pass through a sieve into another pan.

~ Whisk the egg yolks, sugar and honey together, followed by the cornflour.

~ Return the milk to the boil, then whisk half of it into the yolk mixture, then return this to the milk in the pan.

~ Heat until thickened, whisking constantly; it should come to the boil to cook out the cornflour.

~ Pass through a sieve into a bowl and top directly with greaseproof paper, to stop a skin from forming. Cool, then chill in the refrigerator.

~ Once cold and set, beat with a whisk until smooth, then fold in the cream. Return to the refrigerator.

ASSEMBLE

~ Place 2 tablespoons of pastry cream in each pastry case. If using strawberry purée, spoon 1 tablespoon into each case and ripple it through the cream.

~ Scatter over the wild strawberries and lavender, then add the petals, 3–5 per tart, inserting them to give height.

~ Dust lightly with icing sugar.

~ Place ½ teaspoon pastry cream under each tart to stop it sliding on the plate.

SWEET POTATO CAKE, CHARRED PINK GRAPEFRUIT, HONEY & RICOTTA

246

Think of this as an exotic carrot cake! It is moist and soft. The argan oil adds a nutty depth and works brilliantly with the sweet potato and spices.

Serves 8

CAKE

225g argan oil, plus more for the tin

3 large eggs

210g soft brown sugar

225g plain flour

75g ground almonds

1 teaspoon baking powder

1 teaspoon bicarbonate of soda

2 teaspoons ground cinnamon

2 teaspoons mixed spice

pinch of fine sea salt

300g sweet potato, finely grated

finely grated zest of 1 orange

HONEY & RICOTTA

250g ricotta

150g thick Greek yogurt

150g mascarpone

100g clear honey

GRAPEFRUIT

2 pink grapefruits, segmented (page 69)

ASSEMBLE

4 tablespoons chopped pistachios

CAKE

~ Preheat the oven to 170°C. Oil and fully line a 24cm cake tin.

~ In a food mixer, beat the eggs and sugar. Add the oil in a steady stream.

~ Sift together the dry ingredients in a bowl, then whisk into the egg mixture. Mix in the sweet potato and zest.

~ Pour into the prepared tin. Bake for 45 minutes, or until a skewer comes out clean. Remove from the oven, leave to cool for 15 minutes, then turn out on to a wire rack, upside down, so the flat base becomes the cake's top.

HONEY & RICOTTA

~ Whisk all the ingredients together just to combine; do not overwork.

GRAPEFRUIT

~ Place the segments on kitchen paper to dry totally. Transfer to a metal tray.

~ Blowtorch quickly on both sides, or scorch in a hot dry frying pan.

ASSEMBLE

~ Halve the cake horizontally. Spread one-third of the ricotta on the base, place the other cake half on top and spread ricotta over the top and sides.

~ Scatter all over with the pistachios, lightly pressing them into the sides, followed by the grapefruit segments.

RASPBERRY RIPPLE & VANILLA RICE PUDDING

248

The ultimate nursery food, rice pudding is the nourishment that bookends our existence: it is the food of both the very young and the very old. It is loved by those with milk teeth and false teeth alike... and by most people in between. I love it both chilled, as here, and warm, but they are two very different desserts.

This version is just lightly sweetened, with a pure vanilla flavour pervading the rich dairy. In the winter, serve it with soaked prunes, gingerbread crumbs and dulche de leche instead of berries. For a tray-baked version, mix everything as below, adding a couple of knobs of salted butter and a generous grating of nutmeg. Bake at 150°C for 2 hours, stirring after 40 minutes and again after a further 40 minutes, then leave at the end for the rich milk skin to develop. It is both the simplest of desserts and the most rewarding.

RICE PUDDING

1 litre whole milk

100g caster sugar

150g short-grain pudding rice

1 vanilla pod, split lengthways, seeds scraped out

300g whipping cream, whipped to medium peaks

ASSEMBLE

200g raspberries

1 tablespoon icing sugar, or as needed

RICE PUDDING

~ Put the milk, sugar, rice and vanilla seeds and pod in a heavy-based pan and simmer gently for 45 minutes, stirring regularly, until the milk is reduced and the rice is cooked.

~ Pour into a bowl and chill.

~ Once chilled, remove the vanilla pod, then fold in the cream. Chill again, along with 4 serving glasses.

ASSEMBLE

~ Take half the raspberries and crush them with the icing sugar. Check for sweetness and acidity, adjusting the level of sweetness with more icing sugar if needed.

~ Mix the remaining raspberries into the crushed fruit, reserving the 4 best shaped for serving.

~ Add the crushed raspberry sauce to the chilled rice pudding and very loosely marble it in.

~ Transfer to the chilled glasses and top each with a whole perfect raspberry.

GARDEN CUPCAKES

These are absolutely delicious: buttery and rich, but balanced by the acidity of the cooked raspberries within.

The topping is by no means a regular frosting, which is usually just made by whisking butter and sugar and invariably tastes overly sweet and childish. This version is based on mascarpone and yogurt and is only lightly sweetened, creating something far more palatable and refined. The orange blossom, along with the orange zest, give a delicious subtle fragrance.

The herbs and flowers you use to decorate the cakes are completely up to you and obviously dependent on what (unsprayed, untreated) herbs and edible flowers you can get your hands on. You can just keep adding these; unusually for me, restraint goes out the window in this instance. More is more.

Makes 8

CAKES

200g salted butter, plus more, melted, for the cake cases

220g icing sugar

80g plain flour

2 teaspoons baking powder

150g ground almonds

200g egg whites

24 raspberries

FROSTING

250g mascarpone

120g strained Greek yogurt

80g extra thick or regular double cream, whipped to firm peaks

50g icing sugar, sifted

finely grated zest of ½ orange

1 teaspoon orange blossom water

ASSEMBLE

icing sugar

mixed herbs, edible blossoms and petals

CAKES

~ Heat the butter in a saucepan over a medium heat. Wait for it to stop foaming, then keep an eagle eye on it, swirling occasionally and stirring the base of the pan regularly, until it is filled with flecks of a hazelnut colour and the butter smells nutty. This is *beurre noisette*: brown butter.

~ Once it is a nice deep golden, pour it into a bowl, including the sediment, to cool to room temperature.

~ Sift the icing sugar, flour and baking powder into the bowl of a food mixer fitted with the whisk attachment, then stir in the almonds.

~ Gradually whisk in the brown butter, then follow, again gradually, with the egg whites. Chill for 1 hour.

~ Preheat the oven to 190°C. Line a muffin tin with 8 paper cases and brush them with melted butter.

~ Fill each case one-quarter full with the batter, then push 3 raspberries into the centre of each (the cake will rise and, as it does, the raspberries will be pushed outwards). Add more batter until each case is three-quarters full.

~ Bake for 15 minutes, then leave to cool for 5 minutes. Remove the cakes from the trays and paper cases and leave them upside down on a wire rack. This will flatten the tops slightly, which will make the piping easier.

FROSTING

~ Carefully and lightly whisk everything together until combined, with a folding rather than a beating motion. (Mascarpone and yogurt become runny if over-whisked and the mix should remain firm.)

~ Transfer to a piping bag fitted with a star-shaped nozzle, if you have one. Leave to chill in the refrigerator.

ASSEMBLE

~ Dust the cakes, wider flat-side up, with icing sugar.

~ Pipe the frosting generously on top, squeezing the bag a bit firmer than you think you would need to; it is actually easier to pipe if the frosting comes out a little speedily.

~ Insert the herbs and flowers on top, creating height and volume, then serve straightaway.

LEMON VERBENA POSSET, FRAGRANT HERBS

Lemon posset is the simplest dessert: essentially a combination of boiling cream, sugar and lemon juice creates a mix that sets naturally when chilled. It can often, however, be simultaneously too fatty, too sharp and too sweet. This recipe is beautifully balanced. The Chardonnay vinegar gives it an adult edge and the verbena a delicious sherbet-like effervescence. Bruise the verbena just before it goes into the pan, for maximum fragrance. If it's unavailable, use a smaller amount of dried lemon verbena, or substitute 4 lemon grass stalks, bruised and chopped. The mint and marjoram add a pop and turn a classic dessert into something more intriguing, though you can use just one type of herb, or replace them with summer berries if you prefer.

This single recipe encapsulates what I am trying to achieve in this book perhaps better than any other: how a professional mindset can elevate a base recipe into something elegant, yet still recognisably home-cooking, with minimal stress, shopping or clearing up.

POSSET

700g double cream

150g caster sugar

finely grated zest and juice of 2 lemons
(you need 60g lemon juice)

1 teaspoon Chardonnay vinegar

8 lemon verbena sprigs, bruised
(or see recipe introduction)

ASSEMBLE

255

2 marjoram sprigs, leaves picked
(or see recipe introduction)

2 mint sprigs, leaves picked
(or see recipe introduction)

2 lemon verbena sprigs, leaves picked

———

POSSET

~ Place the cream and sugar in a saucepan and bring to the boil.

~ Add the remaining ingredients, reserving one-quarter of the grated lemon zest, and simmer gently for 3 minutes.

~ Remove from the heat and infuse for 30 minutes, then pass through a sieve into a jug and stir in the remaining lemon zest.

~ Divide between 4 bowls or shallow dishes, cover with cling film (don't let it touch the surface of the posset) and leave to chill and set in the refrigerator for no less than 4 hours.

ASSEMBLE

~ Scatter the herbs organically over the posset – without symmetry or pattern, as if they had just fallen naturally – and serve immediately.

PRUNE, APPLE & NUTMEG CLAFOUTIS

The reaction of people when they eat this is one of total surrender and comfort… the pudding equivalent of slipping into a warm bath. This version, somewhere between a custard and a cake, is definitely for a cold autumn evening.

Serves 8

CLAFOUTIS

300g whole milk

200g whipping cream

200g salted butter, plus 25g for the tin

½ vanilla pod, split, seeds scraped out

⅛ nutmeg, grated

1 large egg, plus 3 egg yolks

150g caster sugar

100g plain flour

100g ground almonds

4 tablespoons Demerara sugar

12 prunes, halved, soaked in hot tea for 30 minutes, then drained

2 Braeburn apples, peeled and quartered, each quarter chopped in half

3 tablespoons flaked almonds, toasted (see page 19)

1 tablespoon thyme leaves

ASSEMBLE

finely grated zest of ½ lemon

1 tablespoon icing sugar

300g crème fraîche

CLAFOUTIS

~ Bring the milk, cream and 200g of butter to a simmer in a saucepan, then remove from the heat, add the vanilla pod and seeds and the nutmeg and cover. Leave to infuse for 30 minutes, then pass through a sieve into a bowl.

~ Preheat the oven to 180°C.

~ In a bowl, beat the egg, egg yolks, caster sugar, flour and almonds until smooth; the mixture will be stiff. Add the infused milk in a gradual stream, beating all the time, to form a thick batter.

~ Rub the 25g butter all over the inside of a 26–30cm wide ovenproof dish at least 4cm deep, then scatter with the Demerara sugar to cover completely, shaking off excess. (It looks like a lot, but it forms a delicious crust.)

~ Pour the batter into the cake tin to come two-thirds of the way up, then scatter the fruits evenly within this. Pour over the remaining batter. Bake for 25 minutes, or until set.

~ Scatter over the almonds and thyme and bake for another 3 minutes until lightly toasted.

ASSEMBLE

~ Leave to cool until just warm, then dust over a little lemon zest and icing sugar. Serve with crème fraîche.

STRAWBERRY & BASIL CHARLOTTE

258

A jaunty take on a classic dish. A bowl of strawberry mousse and a dish of strawberries and cream contain pretty much the same ingredients, but are two very different things. This is because the blending of cream into strawberries — as in a mousse — dulls their fragrance, yet eating both together unblended actually highlights the delicious contrast between sweetened dairy and ripe fruit, each bringing out the best in the other. This charlotte is fun to make, striking to look at and delicious to eat. There is a bit of work involved, but the result is well worth it.

VANILLA MASCARPONE

100g whole milk

1 vanilla pod, halved lengthways, seeds scraped out

6 egg yolks

100g caster sugar

4 gelatine leaves, soaked for 10 minutes in iced water, then squeezed out

500g mascarpone

300g double cream, whipped to firm peaks

SOAKING SYRUP

125g caster sugar

10g fruit-flavoured tea, such as Mariage Frères 'Marco Polo'

juice of ½ lemon

STRAWBERRIES

400g strawberries

1 tablespoon icing sugar

ASSEMBLE

12 lady finger biscuits, trimmed to the height of the mugs

24 small basil leaves

4 whole, perfect strawberries

VANILLA MASCARPONE

~ Take 4 large straight-sided mugs or ring moulds, 10cm in diameter, and place in the freezer.

~ Bring the milk to the boil, add the vanilla pod and seeds, remove from the heat and leave for 15 minutes.

~ Whisk the egg yolks and sugar together in a bowl, then whisk in the milk.

~ Return to the heat to thicken, whisking constantly as you would a custard (cook until it reaches 84°C), then remove from the heat and add the soaked and squeezed-out gelatine, stirring until it has dissolved.

~ Pass through a sieve and let it cool to room temperature, then whisk it into the mascarpone, just until combined.

~ Fold in the cream, then chill in the refrigerator.

SOAKING SYRUP

~ Bring 500g water and the sugar to the boil in a saucepan, then remove from the heat, add the tea and lemon juice and pour into a heatproof container. Cover and infuse for 2 minutes, setting a timer.

~ Check the flavour is strong enough but not tannic, then pass through a sieve into a clean bowl.

~ Cool to room temperature, then pour into a shallow dish.

STRAWBERRIES

~ Slice 200g of the strawberries; set aside. Blend the other 200g in a bowl with the icing sugar and 2 tablespoons water, then pass through a sieve.

ASSEMBLE

~ Take the mugs or moulds one at a time and, working quickly, spread some cream around the bottom and sides.

~ Soak the sponge fingers in the syrup so they soften and absorb it but retain their shape and structure (no more than 1 minute), then stick them in the mugs by pushing them to the sides.

~ Spoon or pipe in the rest of the cream to fill, then chill for at least 4 hours.

~ Remove from the refrigerator. Boil a full kettle and fill both a small saucepan and a deep, flat-bottomed bowl with boiling water.

~ Dip a sharp, thin-bladed knife into the pan of hot water, then run this around the outside of the charlottes. Dip the mugs in the deep bowl of hot water for 20 seconds, then unmould each on to a serving plate, allowing gravity to help. If using ring moulds, a quick flash with a blowtorch or just your warm hands will do the job.

~ Place the sliced strawberries and basil around the outside and a perfect berry on top. Serve with the sauce.

SUGAR &

HONEY

At home, we crave 'pudding' rather than 'dessert': something substantial and satisfying rather than a light and airy cheffy creation. I've yet to meet anyone who sprawls on the sofa after a heavy night craving a bowl of fruit soup… When we cook puddings at home, we are propelled by a sense of gluttony towards sugary fulfilment; we hunger for a slice of cheesecake, or a wedge of treacle tart.

Puddings are inherently sweet, but they shouldn't be cloyingly so. As with salt, too much sugar can actually mask other flavours rather than elevating them. After cereals and vegetable oils, sugar provides, on average, the most calories we eat every day. But I think that puddings should be a treat rather than a daily occurrence, or you lose the sense of enjoyment of them.

The sweets here are classic, or at least contemporary twists, and making them will teach you different techniques. Learn how to master a perfectly chewy meringue; addictive madeleines, crisp on the outside and buttery within; moist French toast bathed for hours in custard; silky smooth cheesecake with a crunchy base and the perfect ratio of acidity to richness. The gingerbread custard with Earl Grey meringue is a 'tea and cake' version of queen of puddings. Similarly, adding white miso and apple to treacle tart transforms a garishly sweet and one-dimensional pudding into a far more balanced and sophisticated dish.

Just as savoury cooking often needs the judicious addition of sweetness to balance it, sugar and honey sometimes need salt and acidity. Salt is obligatory for any baked goods or preparations using chocolate or caramel. Its absence is always more noticeable than its presence. Likewise, herbs are sometimes a forgotten ingredient at the end of a meal and can offer a welcome lift when you are feeling at your most satiated and jaded. A pop of fragrant leaves such as mint, basil, marjoram or lemon thyme will provide welcome relief and remind you that gluttony and sophistication can co-exist. Don't be afraid of some of the more floral ingredients used here, such as orange or cherry blossom; they are always included with a light touch.

The variety of sugar that you choose is important. Dark muscovado and molasses carry very grown-up flavours with deep aniseed overtones. Golden caster sugar adds a rounded warmth to cakes, while regular caster sugar should be used when its unsophisticated sweetness will not interfere with the intrinsic delicate flavours in a dessert.

Honey can vary greatly, depending on the type you choose: from light to dark, floral to musky. There are so many interesting honeys available online. The sweetness of honey is fuller and somehow more radiant than that of sugar, so a little goes a long way… which is just as well, as the average honeybee produces only a fraction of a teaspoon of honey in their lifetime. To make 500g, nearly a thousand bees will have to visit nearly two million flowers! That's something to chew on when next spreading it on your toast… Sometimes the small miracles in life can go unnoticed by the ease with which they can be procured.

Whenever cooking a dessert, think about what you will be serving before it, so you make something people actually want to eat. That said, 'the pudding stomach' is definitely a real thing. It is derived from sensory boredom – the desire for something new – which creates appetite. Our stomach and physiology are capable of absorbing nutrients, calories and energy to excess, originally no doubt to act as a biological survival mechanism over winter. Furthermore, the glucose molecules in sugar stimulate relaxation within the stomach, which in turn decreases pressure on it, reducing the sensation of being full. A pudding, in other words, effectively enables the stomach to make more room for it!

Baking is great way to get kids interested in cooking; aged six, the first dish I ever made was profiteroles. Messing about in the kitchen with sweet things is potentially less hazardous for small hands than cooking with raw meat or fish, and often fewer sharp instruments are involved, too.

More importantly, however, there is a greater sense of alchemy and wonder at the end of the process: pedestrian ingredients such as butter, sugar, eggs and flour combine and transform to become so much more than the sum of their parts.

It was what first motivated me to roll up my sleeves and put on an apron…

FRESHLY BAKED MADELEINES, CHANTILLY CREAM

I remember when these first went on the menu at my restaurant, we became known as 'the madeleine place'. None of the other desserts sold; everyone just wanted these. There are a few things that make them such a hit. They are crisp on the outside and buttery within. Tonka beans give them a bitter almond taste and the salt content is on the adult side. You will need two madeleine trays, or you can halve the recipe.

Makes about 30

MADELEINES

250g salted butter plus more for the tins

100g ground almonds

250g icing sugar, plus more to dust

75g plain flour, plus more to dust

250g egg whites

5 tonka beans, finely grated

CREAM

½ vanilla pod (ideally Tahitian)

300g whipping cream

30g caster sugar

___

MADELEINES

~ Heat the butter to noisette (see page 251). Pour into a bowl, including the sediment. Cool to room temperature.

~ Sift the almonds, sugar and flour and gradually whisk in the egg whites.

~ Using a stick blender, gradually blend in the first 20 per cent of the browned butter to emulsify, then add the remainder by hand with a whisk, beating fast and adding the butter slowly, as if making a mayonnaise.

~ Finally, whisk in the tonka beans, then transfer to a piping bag and chill in the refrigerator for a couple of hours.

~ Preheat the oven to 190–200°C and place 2 baking trays inside.

~ Pipe the madeleine mix from cold into very well buttered and floured madeleine tins, then place these in the oven on top of the hot baking trays.

~ Cook for 10–12 minutes, until just cooked, then remove and leave to cool for 2 minutes in the tins.

~ Turn upside down and tap firmly to remove them from the moulds. Dust the scalloped sides with icing sugar.

CREAM

~ Halve the vanilla pod lengthways, scrape out the seeds and mix into the cream. Leave overnight to infuse.

~ Add the sugar and whip to soft peaks. Divide between 4 serving pots.

TO SERVE

~ Serve the madeleines in their trays, or in a bowl lined with a napkin, giving everyone their own pot of cream.

SOAKED ORANGE BLOSSOM CAKE WITH OLIVE OIL

During a holiday in Milos, we ate amazing cakes for breakfast at our hotel, made by the mother of the lady that ran it. They were very different to anything I'd tried before. One day I woke at 5am to see her bake, her daughter translating, and I hope she would approve of my version. Don't be afraid by its randomness!

Serves 8—10

FILO BASE

75g extra virgin olive oil
150g filo pastry
40g caster sugar

FILLING

3 eggs
120g caster sugar
1 teaspoon baking powder
120g extra virgin olive oil, more to serve
240g Greek yogurt, plus 500g to serve
grated zest of 1 orange, more to serve
30g filo pastry, cut into julienne

ORANGE BLOSSOM SYRUP

175g caster sugar
200g orange juice
25g orange blossom water

ASSEMBLE

1 tablespoon coriander seeds, lightly toasted (see page 19) and crushed

FILO BASE

~ Preheat the oven to 170°C. Brush a 26cm cake tin with olive oil.

~ Brush the filo with oil and sprinkle with sugar on both sides, then fold like an accordion and place ruffled-side up in the tin. Bake for 20 minutes.

FILLING

~ Meanwhile, whisk the eggs, sugar and baking powder until thick and fluffy.

~ Gradually add the oil to emulsify, then lightly whisk in the 240g yogurt and zest. Finally, mix in the julienned filo.

~ Remove the baked filo from the cake tin and pour in half the batter. Return the baked filo, pushing it down, then pour in the remaining batter. Crush the filo lightly, so the mix can sink in.

~ Bake for 20 minutes, until light gold and set. Leave to cool.

ORANGE BLOSSOM SYRUP

~ Bring everything to the boil with 300g water. Pour over the cake and leave to soak for at least 2 hours, or overnight.

ASSEMBLE

~ Slice the cake and arrange the slices in a serving bowl. Drizzle with oil, then spread the 500g yogurt over to cover.

~ Grate over some orange zest, then sprinkle lightly with coriander seeds.

BAKED MILK CURDS WITH CHERRY BLOSSOM & SUGARED ALMONDS

This recipe originated from a friend who watched paneer being made in his favourite Indian restaurant. In this dessert, the cultures in the yogurt thicken the mix, which is lightly sweetened and infused with cherry blossom tea. Whenever infusing liquids with teas or herbs, always be wary of time: too long and the tannins can build up to create an unpleasant bitterness. The cherry blossom tea has an amazing and delicate flavour, and is great added to custards or panna cottas.

500g whole milk

100g double cream

400g condensed milk

12g cherry blossom tea (Mariage Frères make a good version)

400g Greek yogurt

8 sugared almonds, roughly chopped

~ Preheat the oven to 90°C.

~ Bring the whole milk and cream to the boil in a saucepan, then remove from the heat and add the condensed milk. Whisk and return to a simmer.

~ Add the tea, cover with a lid and remove from the heat; infuse for 2 minutes only (set a timer).

~ Pass through a sieve into a bowl, then cool to room temperature and whisk into the Greek yogurt.

~ Pour into 4 individual bowls or a large communal one, cover with cling film, then place in a roasting tray lined with a clean, old tea towel. Boil a kettle, then pour enough just-boiled water into the roasting tray to come halfway up the sides of the bowls.

~ Cook for 45 minutes to 1 hour, until just set.

~ Cool to room temperature, then chill overnight in the refrigerator.

~ Scatter with the sugared almonds, then serve.

PANETTONE FRENCH TOAST, ORANGE ZEST & CRÈME FRAÎCHE

There are a few key elements to great French toast. First, use a buttery enriched loaf, such as brioche or panettone. Second, make sure each slice has a crust all around it, as this will help it support its own weight after soaking in the rich, custard-like mix. Third, soak it very well and for longer than you might expect, without any compression, for the fluffiest toasts. Finally, when frying, treat it with kid gloves to keep as much moisture within as possible.

The end result is warm and juicy and the outside caramelised with Demerara sugar, salted butter and rum, to add a grown-up edge.

Serves 8

FRENCH TOAST

6 egg yolks

40g caster sugar

200g whole milk

200g whipping cream

½ vanilla pod, split lengthways, seeds scraped out

8 x 2.5cm-thick slices of panettone

ASSEMBLE

4 tablespoons Demerara sugar

50g salted butter

4 tablespoons rum or Marsala

finely grated zest of 1 orange

300g crème fraîche

FRENCH TOAST

- Beat the egg yolks and sugar in a heatproof bowl, just to combine.

- Bring the milk and cream to the boil, then add the vanilla and pour on to the egg mix, whisking all the time. Cover and cool to room temperature.

- Pour through a sieve into a roasting tray and place the panettone in it.

- Leave for 1 hour, then flip over and soak for another hour.

ASSEMBLE

~ Preheat the oven to 150°C.

~ Using a palette knife, carefully remove the panettone from the soaking mix and sit it on a wire cake rack set over a roasting tin. Don't squeeze the slices; you want them as juicy as possible.

~ Sprinkle the Demerara sugar on the top of the soaked panettone.

~ Colour three-quarters of the salted butter in a nonstick ovenproof frying pan to a light nut-brown.

~ Add all the panettone and colour until golden on one side, adding more butter if needed. Flip over, then place in the oven for 5 minutes.

~ Drizzle over a little rum or Marsala, then place on kitchen paper. Grate over a little orange zest and serve with a generous spoon of crème fraîche.

FRESH RICOTTA WITH APPLES, HAZELNUTS, LEMON THYME, HONEY & VIRGIN RAPESEED OIL

Very much a breakfast or brunch dish, this tastes both nourishing and healthy. It is really important to halve the hazelnuts rather than crush them, as the crunch they bring is key to the recipe. The syrup for the apples is an old recipe of mine and can be used for poaching quince and pears, or rehydrating dried fruits. In the summer, swap apples for apricots.

I use Golden Delicious apples here because they absorb the liquor, but keep their structure, rather than turning into a mush.

SOAKED APPLES

125g moscatel or other dessert wine

1 tablespoon clear honey

1 tablespoon caster sugar

finely grated zest and juice of ½ lemon

½ vanilla pod, halved lengthways, seeds scraped out

1 cardamon pod, crushed

pinch of powdered saffron

4 Golden Delicious apples, peeled

ASSEMBLE

100g hazelnuts

500g fresh ricotta

6 tablespoons whipping cream

4 tablespoons lemon thyme leaves

4 tablespoons virgin rapeseed oil

fine sea salt

SOAKED APPLES

~ Boil the moscatel in a saucepan for 30 seconds, then add 200g water and all the other ingredients except the apples. Return to the boil, then leave to cool to room temperature.

~ Quarter and core the apples. Slice finely lengthways into 2mm slices with a sharp knife or on a mandolin. Place in the moscatel syrup overnight.

ASSEMBLE

~ Preheat the oven to 170°C and spread the hazelnuts out on a tray. Toast in the oven for 10 minutes, then remove and let cool to room temperature. Halve, then lightly season with salt.

~ Mix the ricotta with the cream and season very lightly with salt. Place 130g of the ricotta mixture in the base of each of 4 shallow bowls.

~ Top each with 1 tablespoon hazelnut halves, a spoon of the apple syrup and a pinch of lemon thyme.

~ Drain the apple slices and sit them on top, neatly overlapping.

~ Spoon another 1 tablespoon of the syrup over each and marble with 1 tablespoon virgin rapeseed oil.

~ Scatter over some more hazelnut halves and lemon thyme to serve.

SOFT MERINGUE WITH ALMOND MILK, LEMON BALM & ROAST APRICOTS

The best meringue is crunchy on the outside but soft and chewy within, and this recipe will get you that result every time. Orgeat is an almond syrup more often found in France than here, but it is easily available online and keeps well, due to its sugar content.

The combination of the meringue, almond cream, apricots and lemon balm is absolutely delicious, while the Greek yogurt prevents the dish from becoming too cloying.

There is usually a sadly narrow window for apricots in the summer, and their quality can be variable, so feel free to use mirabelles, greengages or gooseberries instead.

MERINGUE

150g egg whites

150g caster sugar

1 teaspoon cornflour

10g lemon juice (about ¼ of a juicy lemon)

pinch of fine sea salt

APRICOTS

6 apricots, halved and pitted

2 tablespoons caster sugar

3 tablespoons extra virgin olive oil

3 tablespoons moscatel or any other dessert wine (if unavailable, just omit)

ALMOND MILK CREAM

50g orgeat syrup

250g mascarpone

100g thick Greek yogurt

150g whipping cream, whipped to firm peaks

ASSEMBLE

4 tablespoons apricot jam

lemon balm leaves

yellow tagetes or marigold flowers (optional)

MERINGUE

~ Preheat the oven to 110°C.

~ Whisk the egg whites to soft peaks, then gradually add the sugar, while still whisking.

~ Mix the cornflour and lemon juice in a small cup until smooth. Add the salt to the meringue, followed by the cornflour solution, and keep beating for another minute.

~ Take spoons of the meringue and spread on to baking trays lined with greaseproof paper, to create free-form shards, each about 1cm thick and 10–12cm wide. You need 12 in total, plus a couple spare, in case of breakages (they are fragile).

~ Bake for 20 minutes, then reduce the oven temperature to 90°C and cook for a final 30 minutes.

~ Leave to cool, then remove from the baking trays.

APRICOTS

~ Preheat the oven to 150°C.

~ Mix everything together in a roasting tray and roast for 10–12 minutes, until the apricots are tender but still holding their shape.

~ Remove from the oven and leave to cool to room temperature.

ALMOND MILK CREAM

~ Lightly whisk the orgeat syrup into the mascarpone in a bowl, then fold in the yogurt, followed by the cream. Chill until needed.

ASSEMBLE

~ Mix any juices from roasting the apricots into the apricot jam.

~ For each plate, spoon a blob of the cream on the bottom, then top with a meringue shard.

~ Top with more cream, a roast apricot half, ½ tablespoon jam and some lemon balm, then repeat to create a jaunty stack, finally topping with a third meringue shard.

~ Scatter over some tagetes or marigold flowers, if using.

WHITE MISO TREACLE TART, FENNEL SEED CRÈME FRAÎCHE

Treacle tart is something I've always enjoyed, but, even as a child, I found its sweetness overbearing. Perhaps that's hardly surprising given that, at its most basic, the filling consists of nothing more than golden syrup and white breadcrumbs. This recipe came from a desire to make it a bit more refined, leading me to add apple, miso, ginger and black treacle, though with a judicious hand, so it irrefutably still feels like treacle tart. This is also lighter and more moist than the classic. Treacle tart is delicious with plain pouring cream, if you want to skip the fennel seed crème fraîche.

Serves 8

TART

30g brown butter (see page 251), made from 50g salted butter, then cooled

25g milk

1 egg, lightly beaten

16g white miso paste

16g black treacle

180g golden syrup

½ teaspoon ground ginger

finely grated zest and juice of ½ lemon

120g brown sourdough bread, blended to crumbs (with crusts is fine)

1 Braeburn apple, skin-on, grated, avoiding the core

1 Wholemeal pastry case (see page 302)

CRÈME FRAÎCHE

400g crème fraîche

1 tablespoon fennel seeds, toasted (see page 19) and lightly crushed

finely grated zest of ¼ lemon

———

TART

~ Preheat the oven to 150°C.

~ Mix everything together (except the pastry case!).

~ Fill the pastry case, then bake for 25 minutes, until the filling is set and golden all over.

~ Remove from the oven and leave to cool for about 10 minutes.

CRÈME FRAÎCHE

~ Mix everything just to combine and leave for a couple of hours to allow the flavours to develop.

TO SERVE

~ Serve slices of still-warm tart with a healthy dollop of the crème fraîche.

WARM GINGERBREAD & EARL GREY PUDDING

Tea and cake, but not as you know it. This combination of bergamot from the tea with the ginger is delicious, while serving it warm and soft, just out the oven, adds a level of indulgence and comfort. It is definitely best served when it's cold outside. Only seven ingredients needed here! The egg yolks go into the custard, the whites into the meringue.

GINGERBREAD CUSTARD

250g whole milk

250g whipping cream

6 egg yolks

65g caster sugar

140g Jamaican ginger cake, or gingerbread, chopped

EARL GREY MERINGUE

1 Earl Grey teabag

120g caster sugar

3 egg whites

finely grated zest of ½ pink grapefruit

———

GINGERBREAD CUSTARD

~ Preheat the oven to 140°C. Bring the milk and cream to the boil in a pan.

~ Whisk the egg yolks and sugar in a heatproof bowl, then whisk in the hot milk. Pour into a blender and blend in the cake or gingerbread.

~ Place a clean tea towel in a roasting tray and sit 4 teacups within.

~ Pour the custard into these to come three-quarters of the way up and individually cover with cling film. Fill the tray to halfway up the cups with just-boiled water from a kettle.

~ Bake for 30 minutes until just set. Remove from the oven and from the water bath, then remove the cling film. As soon as the custard comes out of the oven, start on the meringue.

EARL GREY MERINGUE

~ Make a cup of tea with 100g water and the teabag, infusing it for 3 minutes. Pour this into a saucepan, removing the teabag.

~ Add the sugar and cook over a medium-high heat until it reaches 121°C on a thermometer.

~ Separately whisk the egg whites to soft peaks in a food mixer, then slowly beat in the sugar syrup, trying to avoid the beater, until shiny and stiff. Add the zest and mix well.

~ Transfer to a piping bag, then pipe the meringue on to the custard, or just spoon it on in a swirly shape.

~ Blowtorch to colour the meringue all over, or place under a preheated hot grill, then serve while still warm.

VANILLA CHEESECAKE

I love the balance of this cheesecake. Not too dry or lactic, not too sweet, and the richness just offset by the addition of yogurt. Two varieties of yogurt are used to achieve this: Greek yogurt provides richness, while regular yogurt brings the sharpness, but, if needed, just use a single variety. If you ever make a cheesecake recipe, do give this a go. I think that not baking the cheesecake gives a lighter texture and a smoother result. The vanilla is also key: use Tahitian if at all possible, it is worth every penny. Feel free to decorate with any fresh fruit of your choice, though it is also worth trying the cheesecake unadorned.

Serves 8 generously

265g Hobnobs, or other sweet oaty biscuits

115g unsalted butter, melted

750g Philadelphia cream cheese

250g mascarpone

200g Greek yogurt

200g regular natural yogurt (not set)

250g icing sugar

150g whipping cream

1 vanilla pod (ideally Tahitian), split lengthways, seeds scraped out

4 gelatine leaves, soaked for 10 minutes in iced water, then squeezeed out

red and black fresh fruits, or finely grated lemon zest, to serve (optional)

~ Blitz the biscuits with the butter in a food processor. Press evenly and firmly into a loose-based 26–28cm cake tin, then chill.

~ Beat the cream cheese, mascarpone, both yogurts and the icing sugar in a large bowl just until smooth. Don't take it too far, as mascarpone and yogurt become runny if over-whisked and the mix should remain firm.

~ Warm the cream in a saucepan, then add the vanilla pod and seeds, remove from the heat and infuse for 15 minutes. Now add the squeezed-out gelatine and whisk it in while the cream is still warm, until dissolved.

~ Pass through a sieve and cool to room temperature, then mix well with the cream cheese mixture.

~ Pour the filling on to the base in the cake tin, cover and chill until set (at least 4 hours).

~ Remove the cheesecake from the tin and slice it into generous segments. I like this completely plain, though it's also great with red or black fruits, or some lemon zest grated over.

CHOCOLATE POT WITH FRAGRANT HERBS

Due to a blockade imposed by Napoleon in the early 19th century, there was a shortage of cocoa in Turin. This led to chocolate being cut with a paste made from hazelnuts, abundant in Piedmont… and gianduja was born. A great thing to come out of a bad situation. Here, it is made into cremeux: lighter than ganache but firmer than a mousse. The 'soil' adds salinity.

CHOCOLATE 'SOIL'

75g salted butter, chilled and chopped

110g ground almonds

75g plain flour

40g cocoa powder

130g caster sugar

large pinch of fine sea salt

GIANDUJA CREMEUX

150g whole milk

150g whipping cream

3 egg yolks

300g dark chocolate gianduja, chopped

pinch of fine sea salt

ASSEMBLE

200g crème fraîche

6 tablespoons toasted whole hazelnuts

leaves from 6 Thai basil sprigs, or regular basil sprigs, plus more to serve

1 teaspoon fennel pollen, or ground fennel seeds

CHOCOLATE 'SOIL'

~ Preheat the oven to 170°C.

~ Mix all the ingredients in a food mixer, or with your fingers, then spread evenly over a tray.

~ Bake for 20 minutes, then leave to cool until crisp.

~ Empty into a bag, then bash with a rolling pin, or chop with a large knife, to break into a fine crumble.

GIANDUJA CREMEUX

~ Bring the milk and cream to the boil, pour one-third of this over the yolks in a bowl, whisking constantly, then return everything to the pan. Cook to 85°C, or until it thickens, stirring constantly, then pass through a sieve.

~ Combine the custard, chocolate and salt, then blend with a hand blender.

~ Chill for 4 hours. Return to room temperature 1 hour before serving.

ASSEMBLE

~ Divide the crème fraîche between 4 pots, top with 3 tablespoons cremeux and smooth with the back of a spoon.

~ Scatter over the hazelnuts and basil.

~ Top with 2 tablespoons each of chocolate soil, followed by a tiny sprinkle of fennel pollen, or seeds. Insert a basil sprig, standing up in the soil as if growing.

STRAINED GREEK YOGURT, CELERY & PEAR, MUSCOVADO & PEPPERMINT

I have friends that would look at this recipe and raise an eyebrow. The yogurt is spread thinly and topped with muscovado, which gives it a lovely depth and aniseed flavour. The celery and pear combine as an elegant fresh salad that works brilliantly alongside it; the mint adds a pop that brings the whole dish to life. This is a great example of a dish that you might not order — in my experience, people generally like to go for chocolate desserts rather than choose anything healthy — but I bet you would really enjoy it if you tried it. That is why tasting menus can be fun... as long as you trust the chef cooking for you!

This is the perfect dish for people who don't really like desserts, as it's not very sweet and tastes very fresh, with herbaceous pops.

SUGARED CELERY

4 celery sticks, peeled of all string

1 tablespoon icing sugar, sifted

juice of ¼ lemon

ASSEMBLE

600g Greek yogurt

4 tablespoons muscovado sugar

2 ripe pears, peeled and sliced into thin wedges

handful of peppermint tips (about 20)

handful of bronze fennel fronds, or dill (about 20)

SUGARED CELERY

~ Peel the celery into thin strips and dress in a bowl with the sugar and lemon juice. Marinate overnight.

ASSEMBLE

~ Place a large dollop of yogurt (about 150g per person) in the centre of each plate and spread into a rough circle.

~ Sprinkle over enough muscovado sugar to lightly cover. Leave for 10 minutes for the sugar to dissolve and 'melt' on top.

~ Scatter the pear wedges, celery strips and herbs on top in an organic manner, creating height and volume. There should be 4–5 sprigs of each herb per person.

LARDER

Larders these days are very much a thing of the past. I remember my grandmother's home in Ruddington, a small village just outside Nottingham, during the late 1980s. Hers was a small semi-detached house with a cool dark cupboard in the kitchen, running under the stairs. Here you would find all the jarred goods and preserves: Ploughman's Pickle, Bird's custard powder, various jams, some walnut whips and maybe a Battenburg cake (this was back when teatime still existed). Nothing fancy, for sure, but this was nonetheless a bonafide cornucopia for a young boy with a sweet tooth and a determined nature. Usually the sugary items would be hidden away, or placed high up on shelves beyond my grasp, especially the packets of dissolvable jelly cubes – usually blackcurrant flavour – which, at seven years old, I loved to eat straight from the packet.

These days, a chilled dark larder full of dry goods is less common, especially in cities, where kitchen space is at a premium. It has been replaced by a cupboard in the kitchen, stacked wildly and to the brim, filled with dried pasta, canned tomatoes, olive oil and breakfast cereal, often dotted with the latest zeitgeist ingredient and its owner's personal idiosyncratic tastes. I think you can tell a lot about a person by what they keep in their storecupboard: definitely, you can tell their age.

Ironically, the word 'larder' today is most often used in professional kitchens, to describe the cold starter section: the team of chefs who make salads, terrines, carpaccios, tartares and the like. Unfortunately, the word 'pantry' is facing extinction in wider society, as the room itself falls out of use in our homes.

But the *concept* of a larder remains essential to the home cook, especially on those days when you don't have anything in the house and don't want to go shopping: you need to be creative and think on your feet. Having flavoursome preparations at your disposal makes daily cooking so much easier and more varied: your get-out-of-jail card to something nutritious and delicious without the need to resort to takeaways (which can sometimes disappoint).

Marinades, pickles and chutneys can all be made in bulk and stored for a long time somewhere cool. And think ahead when you are planning meals. What will keep? Make extra and freeze it. The more laborious the cooking process, the bigger the batch you should make. Keep some stickers and a marker pen for labelling and buy a few airtight containers. You'll save time and money, and your grocery shopping will go a lot further.

The pickles, chutney and marmalade in this chapter have lower acidity and sweetness levels than you would find in classic recipes. This is deliberate and is so that you can still taste the main ingredients, which retain their fresh flavour and integrity rather than descending into an ambiguous mulch, having been stewed for hours with too much vinegar and/or sugar.

The baharat spices here will transform the potentially bland into something exotic and delicious, while the miso, honey and mustard dressing immediately gives an unmistakeable Asian savoury-sweet edge and can be added to just about anything. These bold flavours are great to use when you want to cook up leftovers, or prepare vegetables that are past their best. The breadcrumb dish is also a smart way to utilise what might otherwise be thrown away.

The best cooks are invariably among the most frugal; they love food, so they respect it the most.

DUKKAH

Dukkah is an Egyptian spice mix that perks up just about whatever you sprinkle it on. You can buy it, but it is so easy to make and this recipe is beautifully balanced. It keeps well and is fantastic for adding flavour when you have little time or inclination to be behind the stove.

Makes 350g

125g pine nuts

125g sesame seeds

50g cumin seeds

25g fennel seeds

25g coriander seeds

1 teaspoon chilli flakes or espelette pepper

fine sea salt

~ Toast the nuts and seeds in a hot pan – or in an oven preheated to 180°C – until golden. Grind the pine nuts in a food processor until finely chopped, then remove and place in a bowl.

~ Put the remaining ingredients in the processor, add a pinch of salt and grind to a coarse powder. Add to the nuts.

SESAME LABNEH

Delicious with barbecued meat and fish, especially anything with a Middle Eastern influence. If your Greek yogurt is thick, it will be fine straight from the pot for the labneh. If it is a little thin, then strain it overnight before using. To do this, tip it into a double layer of new J-cloth or muslin and place in a sieve over a bowl, covering the top. Leave to strain and thicken overnight.

Serves 4 as a condiment

125g tahini, at room temperature

2 tablespoons Chardonnay vinegar

finely grated zest and juice of ½ lemon

1 tablespoon clear honey

100g Greek yogurt, strained (see recipe introduction)

fine sea salt

~ Mix 100g water into the tahini to loosen, then whisk in everything else with a pinch of fine sea salt.

LEMON DRESSING

This is a staple of my storecupboard and completely essential to my recipes.

Serves 4 with a salad

juice of 1 lemon (you need 30g here)

2 tablespoons Chardonnay vinegar

1 teaspoon caster sugar

1 teaspoon fine sea salt

200g extra virgin olive oil

~ Place everything in a jam jar with a secure lid, add 2 tablespoons water and shake well to emulsify.

MAYONNAISE

Makes 300g

2 egg yolks, as fresh as possible

1 teaspoon Dijon mustard

juice of ½ lemon

2 tablespoons Chardonnay vinegar

pinch of caster sugar

150g vegetable oil

100g extra virgin rapeseed oil

fine sea salt

~ Place all the ingredients except the oils in a container with a pinch of fine sea salt, add 1 tablespoon water and blend.

~ Blend in the oils gradually until thick and homogenous. Check the seasoning, then chill.

PICCALILLI

This has a lot of ingredients, but it keeps very well and is great to have in your refrigerator.

Makes 1.5kg

300g cider vinegar

75g malt vinegar

4g coriander seeds

4g ground turmeric

4g ground ginger

1 star anise

4g fine sea salt

150g caster sugar

2 garlic cloves, smashed with the side of a knife

30g plain flour

12g mustard powder

1 cauliflower

1 onion, peeled

1 carrot, peeled

100g green beans

15g each dark and white mustard seeds, soaked for 2 hours in boiling water

75g gherkins, chopped

~ Pour both vinegars into a large pan with 150g water, then add the spices, salt, sugar and garlic. Bring to the boil, then reduce by one-third.

~ Pass the vinegar through a sieve into another saucepan over a medium-high heat. Whisk some of it into the flour and mustard powder in a bowl until smooth, then return this to the vinegar in the pan, whisking, while it comes to the boil.

~ Simmer, whisking continuously, for 2–3 minutes, until thickened, then remove from the heat.

~ Cut the cauliflower, onion, carrot and green beans into small (1cm) pieces.

~ Blanch in boiling salted water until just softened but still crunchy, then remove and add to the vinegar pan.

~ Finally, mix in the drained mustard seeds and gherkins. Check the seasoning, spice and acidity. Cool, then chill, potted in sterilised jars if you prefer (see page 304). It should keep indefinitely.

BAHARAT

Makes 100g

Baharat spice elevates any meat or fish, so it's well worth making a bigger batch than you need and keeping it in an airtight container. The cinnamon, nutmeg and cloves make it gentle and warm: very much a North African flavour.

2 tablespoons cumin seeds, toasted (see page 19)

1 tablespoon coriander seeds

1 cinnamon stick

1 teaspoon cardamon pods

1 teaspoon cloves

¼ nutmeg, grated

2 tablespoons sweet paprika

Blitz all the whole spices to a powder, then mix in the nutmeg and paprika.

BREADCRUMBS

Migas *is a dish made in Spain, Portugal and South America, each version with its own character, history and idiosyncracies.* Migas *means breadcrumbs and it is, at its heart, leftover bread fried in oil with different flavours added.*

The variations are endless and the regional differences are no doubt a result of what grows locally. You can take it in many different directions: add chorizo, thyme and piquillo peppers; duck fat, wild mushrooms and chestnuts; or anchovies, garlic and parsley.

This can be a meal in itself or served alongside a poached egg and some salad leaves.

This version is fantastic with roast lamb or chicken, or some crumbled goat's cheese and dressed leaves. Za'atar is a deliciously woody and aromatic herb from the Mediterranean.

Serves 4–6 as a side dish or garnish

200g leftover bread, crusts removed and crumb chopped

150g olive oil

1 garlic clove, crushed

1 tablespoon chopped thyme leaves

150g artichokes in oil (drained weight), halved

100g toasted hazelnuts, lightly crushed or halved

1 tablespoon finely chopped preserved lemon

2 tablespoons za'atar

fine sea salt

_____

~ Blend the bread briefly to achieve a texture somewhere between croutons and coarse breadcrumbs.

~ Fry the crumbs in the olive oil until light golden, controlling the heat and stirring regularly so they colour roughly evenly.

~ Add the garlic and thyme and season lightly, then mix in the remaining ingredients, stirring over the heat just long enough to warm through.

297

ROAST AUBERGINE WITH MISO, HONEY & MUSTARD

I include this recipe in this section because the dressing can be made purely from items found in your storecupboard. It is a go-to solution for a quick supper, and is equally delicious on salmon or chicken. Furthermore, you can make up a big batch of the marinade and keep it indefinitely until needed.

Given how busy people are in general, I would always advise home cooks to build up a store of marinades, dressings, spice mixes, pickles and so on. They are perfect when you are short on time, or feeling uninspired.

Serves 4 as a snack or side dish

MARINADE

2 tablespoons white miso paste

2 tablespoons light soy sauce

1 tablespoon rice wine vinegar (white wine vinegar is also fine)

1 tablespoon Dijon mustard

1 tablespoon clear honey

1 tablespoon caster sugar

½ teaspoon ground ginger

AUBERGINES

2 tablespoons sunflower oil

2 tablespoons toasted sesame oil

2 aubergines, halved and scored criss-cross on the flesh side, lightly salted

4 spring onions

1 small, sweet red chilli, split down the middle and deseeded

2 tablespoons toasted white and black sesame seeds

¼ bunch of coriander leaves

___

MARINADE

~ Whisk together all the ingredients for the marinade with 2 tablespoons water and store in a dark cupboard.

AUBERGINES

~ Heat a large frying pan, then add both the oils and fry the aubergines flesh-side down until golden brown.

~ Turn over and repeat to fry the skin side, then transfer to a baking tray, cut-sides up.

~ Preheat the grill to its highest setting.

~ Spoon about 2 tablespoons marinade over the flesh of each aubergine half and grill for 5–10 minutes, basting throughout, until glazed.

~ Meanwhile, finely slice the spring onions and chilli on the diagonal and keep in some iced water to mellow the flavours and crisp the textures.

~ Scatter the aubergines with the spring onions, chilli, sesame seeds and coriander, then serve.

BAHARAT POT-ROAST CAULIFLOWER

The sesame dressing here is a delicious sauce that can be prepared from relatively few ingredients and keeps well in the refrigerator. If you don't have time to pot-roast the whole cauliflower, cut it into thick steaks through the stem, season with the baharat and pan-fry on both sides, finishing in a hot oven. This would be delicious with Einkorn wheat pilaf (see page 35).

CAULIFLOWER

1 large cauliflower, base trimmed, ideally with some leaves still attached

4 tablespoons virgin rapeseed oil

2 tablespoons Baharat (see page 295), plus more to serve

4 tablespoons salted butter, melted

fine sea salt

SESAME DRESSING

250g tahini, at room temperature

50g Chardonnay vinegar

finely grated zest and juice of 1 lemon

1 small garlic clove, minced

1 tablespoon clear honey

125g Greek yogurt

½ teaspoon fine sea salt

CAULIFLOWER

~ Bring a large saucepan of water to the boil, seasoning it with 20g salt for each 1 litre of water.

~ Add the cauliflower and blanch for 5 minutes, then refresh in iced water. Drain well and place on a tray lined with a new J-cloth to dry.

~ Preheat the oven to 170°C.

~ Place the cauliflower in a casserole that fits it snugly, drizzle generously with the oil and salt it lightly.

~ Sprinkle with the 2 tablespoons of baharat, then cover with a lid.

~ Bake for 45 minutes, then remove the lid and cook for another 45 minutes.

~ Leave to cool slightly, then spoon over the melted butter to glaze the dish and add richness.

SESAME DRESSING

~ Whisk 200g water into the tahini, followed by everything else for the dressing. Keep at room temperature.

TO SERVE

~ Spoon the dressing on a serving plate and top with the cauliflower, or serve the dressing in a bowl alongside, drizzled with the flavoured oil from the casserole and sprinkled with baharat. Serve the cauliflower whole and carve it at the table.

WHOLEMEAL PASTRY CASE

Always handy to have to hand in the freezer.

Makes 1 x 26cm diameter tart case

100g unsalted butter, plus 1 tablespoon
more, softened, for the tin

50g icing sugar

20g muscovado sugar

pinch of fine sea salt

finely grated zest of ¼ lemon

1 large egg, lightly beaten

175g plain flour, plus more to dust

40g wholemeal flour

_____

~ Mix together the butter, icing sugar,
muscovado, salt and lemon zest in
a food mixer fitted with the paddle
attachment. Once everything has
combined, add the egg and mix gently
until combined. Finish by beating in
both flours.

~ Roll into a log about 4cm in diameter,
then wrap in cling film and leave
to rest for at least 12 hours in the
refrigerator before use.

~ Take the dough out of the refrigerator
5 minutes before starting to roll it, to
soften up a little.

~ Roll it out on a floured surface to
3mm thick, then chill once again in
the refrigerator for 1 hour.

~ Remove from the refrigerator and cut
out a ring about 34cm in diameter to
fit a 26cm diameter tart ring or loose-
bottomed tart tin (allow the diameter
of the base plus the height of the sides
as a guide). Return to the refrigerator.
Spread the 1 tablespoon butter around
the tart ring or tin and allow it to set
in the refrigerator for 20 minutes.

~ Line the tart ring with the pastry and
leave to air-dry in the refrigerator for
a couple of hours before cooking.

~ Preheat the oven to 160°C, then place
the tart case in the oven and cook for
15 minutes until light golden.

TOASTED ALMOND, HONEY & ARGAN OIL SPREAD

Amlou is a Moroccan staple and a deliciously grown-up alternative to peanut butter. It's equally wonderful served on toasted bread, porridge, cheese or baked fruits... pretty much whatever you can think of. You could even stir a couple of spoons into a spiced lamb braise, to add depth and richness.

Makes 400g

250g whole blanched almonds

125g argan oil

3 tablespoons clear honey

1 tablespoon brown sugar

½ teaspoon fine sea salt

~ Preheat the oven to 180°C. Spread the almonds out on a tray and toast for 10 minutes, until deep brown.

~ Leave to cool slightly, then blend in a food processor to a paste.

~ Gradually add the oil in a slow steady stream, followed by the honey, sugar and salt.

~ Check the seasoning, then store in a sterilised kilner jar (see page 304). It will keep, chilled, indefinitely.

PICKLED ONIONS

The addition of star anise here dramatically improves the taste of pickled onions. These are beautifully balanced: neither too sweet nor too sharp. You can choose any onion and slice it however you like, but do remember you need to maintain some crunch: pickles are rarely soft, and here their crisp acidity needs to be matched by a crisp texture.

These onions are delicious with smoked fish or cold roast beef, or just added to a green salad. Very quick to make and, like any pickle, worth making in bulk.

Red onions turn almost fluorescent in colour with the addition of the vinegar.

Makes 1kg net weight of pickled onions

500g white wine vinegar

40g fine sea salt

200g caster sugar

4 star anise

1kg red onions, white onions or shallots, peeled

~ To sterilise jars, preheat the oven to 170°C. Wash the jars and lids in hot water with liquid detergent, then rinse well but do not dry with a towel (as that may have bacteria on it).

~ Place on a baking tray and heat for 10 minutes. Place any rubber closures separately in a bowl and cover with boiling water.

~ For the pickled onions, in a saucepan, heat together the vinegar, salt, sugar and star anise with 1 litre water to allow the salt and sugar to dissolve and all the flavourings to infuse.

~ Slice your onions of choice into segments or rings, as you prefer.

~ Blanch the onions in a separate saucepan of simmering water until they just lose their raw taste but are still crunchy; 1–2 minutes, depending on the onion. White onions are the quickest, followed by shallots, then red onions.

~ Strain the onions, transfer to the hot pickle liquor and fill hot, sterilised kilner jars with this to the brim.

~ Seal shut and leave to cool. These will keep indefinitely.

PICKLED QUINCE

Quince poached in dessert wine is a personal favourite of mine. It is delicious as a dessert, but equally so when lightly pickled, as it is here, through the addition of vinegar. The rounded sweetness of the wine and vanilla combine with the honeyed flavour of the quince to create something special. This is delicious with cheese, cold cuts, charcuterie or game.

The amount given in the recipe makes a lot, but you'll never regret having it in your storecupboard.

Makes about 2.5 litres, depending on the size of the quince

750g moscatel dessert wine

60g Chardonnay vinegar

60g caster sugar

pinch of fine sea salt

pinch of crushed black pepper

1 vanilla pod, split lengthways, seeds scraped out

3 fresh bay leaves

8 quince, peeled, cut into wedges or slices, cores removed

———

~ Put everything except the quince in a large saucepan with 375g water and bring to the boil, then add the quince wedges or slices and gently poach for about 15 minutes, until tender but still holding their shape.

~ Sterilise some large pickling jars (see page 304).

~ Place the hot quince and poaching liquid into the hot sterilised jars and seal, then leave to cool. This will keep indefinitely.

TOMATO &
BLACK TREACLE
CHUTNEY

308

Here the black treacle and muscovado sugar lend a bold aniseed flavour to the chutney. The salted butter rounds out the sweet and sour combination, making it smooth and refined rather than aggressive or jarring. The cinnamon is also a warming spice, but you can add cumin seeds if you want something with a bit more poke.

I never add huge amounts of vinegar, sugar or spices to chutneys or relishes as they can mask the main ingredient. This is delicious with cheese, or can be used much like a posh tomato ketchup.

Makes about 2 litres

3 red onions, finely sliced

125g salted butter

1kg ripe tomatoes, cored and chopped

500g cherry tomatoes, halved

½ teaspoon fine sea salt

1 cinnamon stick

1 bay leaf

2 tablespoons muscovado sugar

2 tablespoons black treacle

50g Chardonnay vinegar, or to taste

pinch of chilli flakes

1 tablespoon onion seeds

2 tablespoons cornflour

~ Sweat the onions in the butter in a large saucepan for 10 minutes over a gentle heat, covered. Add all the remaining ingredients, except the cornflour, and simmer for about 45 minutes.

~ Whisk 100g water into the cornflour in a small bowl, then whisk this into the tomato mixture and return to the boil to thicken. Check the seasoning and acidity and adjust if necessary.

~ While still piping hot, place in sterilised hot kilner jars (see page 304) full to the brim and seal shut. Cool and store. This will keep for at least 1 month.

PINK GRAPEFRUIT, JASMINE & OLIVE OIL MARMALADE

This is a labour of love, but it keeps well and makes a great gift. This is a large amount and you can choose to cook half, but if you do you will only regret it when you get to the bottom of the last jar! The flavours here are crystal-clear and quite different to any other jams on the high street shelves. Jasmine and pink grapefruit are a favourite combination of mine, while the olive oil rounds off the acidity and provides a sense of luxury, giving an almost curd-like smoothness. This is definitely best served on wholemeal toast.

Makes 2.5kg, but easily halved if required

8 pink grapefruits

800g caster sugar, plus 250g

8 jasmine teabags

120g lemon juice

24g pectin powder

300g extra virgin olive oil

———

~ Take 2 of the grapefruits, stab each a few times with a paring knife, then place in your largest saucepan.

~ Fill the pan with water, bring to a simmer and cook for 2 hours, then strain. Blend the fruit until smooth and pass the purée through a sieve.

~ Take another 2 grapefruits, trim off the very top and bottom, then remove the skin and pith as if segmenting (see page 69). Julienne the skins and pith; there should be about 75g.

~ Place the julienne in a saucepan with 5 litres cold water (or as much as your biggest saucepan can accommodate), bring to the boil and simmer for 10 minutes. Strain, rinse for 30 seconds, then repeat the process.

~ Segment these 2 grapefruit and the 4 remaining ones over a bowl (see page 69), saving the fibrous cores, then chop each segment into 3.

~ Squeeze all the juice from the cores and keep separately to the segments.

~ Bring 600g water and the 800g sugar to the boil, then remove from the heat and add the teabags. Infuse for 5 minutes, then remove the teabags.

~ Place the fruit purée, julienned skins and pith, grapefruit juice, lemon juice and jasmine syrup in a saucepan and bring to the boil.

~ Add the remaining 250g sugar and the pectin and cook for another 5 minutes, then whisk in the olive oil.

~ Remove from the heat and add the grapefruit segments, stir well to combine without breaking them up too much, then fill up hot sterilised kilner jars (see page 304) to the brim.

~ Seal shut and leave to cool. The marmalade will keep indefinitely.

BELAZU

Beautiful vinegars and oils of all descriptions, from fig leaf-infused olive oil to virgin argan oil. Chardonnay, Cabernet Sauvignon, sherry and apple vinegars are also available, as well as pickled *zahter* (za'atar), einkorn (called *siyez*) and piquillo peppers. A one-stop shop for anything Mediterranean.

www.belazu.com

COTSWOLD GOLD

Virgin and smoked rapeseed oil of a high quality.

www.cotswoldgold.co.uk

FLYING FISH

I first started ordering fish from Johnny when we were both in our early twenties: me a young chef running the fish section at Le Manoir aux Quat' Saisons. Twenty years on, we are both still at the coal face and I remain very proud to buy his fish. The quality is irrefutable, and now you can have it delivered to your door.

www.flyingfishseafoods.co.uk/
flyingfish-at-home

LA FROMAGERIE

Aside from their retail stores in London, La Fromagerie now offer an amazing online deli for home delivery. Great cheeses, but a lot more besides.

www.lafromagerie.co.uk

LE MARCHE DES CHEFS HAMPERS

A restaurant supplier that now offers hampers of fruit and vegetables, meat and fish, sourced from farmers both in the UK and from Rungis market in Paris. Quite simply, the very best restaurant-quality produce, delivered to your door, in a weekly-changing seasonal hamper.

www.lmdc-hampers.co.uk

SOUS CHEF

Just about any random larder ingredient from anywhere in the world can be found here. Use the search engine if looking for something specific, but it's fascinating just to browse the mind-boggling spectrum of products they stock.

www.souschef.co.uk

SUSHI SUSHI

A vast array of Japanese ingredients and serving ware, completely different to any you can find on the supermarket shelves. The koji soy sauce and dashi vinegar are personal favourites.

www.sushisushi.co.uk

WHISKY EXCHANGE

All the liqueurs, fruit purées and syrups (including orgeat) you could ever need are here.

thewhiskyexchange.com

Sincere and heartfelt thanks to my serial partner for works such as this: Joakim Blockström. Such an easy and enjoyable relationship. The results, as always, are amazing. I hope you feel as proud of the book as I do, and I hope that we can find the time to make a couple of these dishes together before too long.

Also to Dave Brown, design editor. Thank you for creating something that has far exceeded my expectations, something that is simultaneously new, individual and organic. It has been a pleasure working with you on this. I couldn't have been in better hands.

To Martin Carabott, senior chef at Hide: thank you for doing such a fantastic job, helping organise all the prep for the many photoshoots. You have characteristically been the model professional throughout. It was a military operation that involved prep for 14 dishes each day, not to mention plenty of loading and unloading. The effortless feel to the photography belies your monumental efforts behind the camera. Also thanks to Zak Poulot, head pastry chef, for your help and enthusiasm.

Thanks to Lucy Bannell, project editor, for elevating my words into the best version of themselves and for probing me to dig out thoughts that I hadn't put into words before. You have created something attainable and homely from an unlikely source!

To Jen Kay, for providing a pitch-perfect supply of plates, backgrounds and various foliage. It has been really fun to work alongside you with this.

And of course to Rowan Yapp, thank you for overseeing it all, granting us freedom of expression and trusting us to deliver a book that feels like a culmination of all our talents. I hope there will be more to come.

Finally, thanks to Josh Angus and all the chefs at Hide for their hard work, professionalism and good will. You do an incredible job, and I am incredibly grateful.

313

320

Ollie Dabbous is the co-founder and executive chef of Hide restaurant in Piccadilly, which was awarded a Michelin star within six months of opening. Hideaway, a café in Mayfair's Mount Street, opened in late 2020. Ollie was previously the Michelin-starred chef-owner of the restaurant Dabbous, famed for its stripped-back fine dining and industrial decor. Ollie has worked at Le Manoir aux Quat' Saisons, Hibiscus, Mugaritz, Noma, L'Astrance, The Fat Duck, WD-50, Pierre Gagnaire and Texture.

He was born in Kuwait and spent some early years there, then came to England to go to school, growing up in Surrey. His French-Italian father was an architect working in the Middle East and his mother a fashion designer working in London. Ollie's honest love of eating and making good food – along with a strong aesthetic – meant he only ever wanted to be a chef.

He says: 'Eating should bring joy above all else. Aside from technical ability, resilience and palate, what is most important as a chef is to know what you like and what you don't and to find a clear style of cooking to express that. Confidence through restraint, and vice versa. I will never sacrifice flavour for gimmickry.

'I want to help you to create something delicious and nourishing for your loved ones, something you will feel proud to serve. Hopefully, this cookbook will be around long after I have hung up my apron.'

Ollie's first book, *Dabbous: The Cookbook*, was published by Bloomsbury in 2014.